Unwin Education Books: *19*

CONCEPTS IN PRIMARY EDUCATION

Unwin Education Books

Series Editor: Ivor Morrish, BD, BA, Dip. Ed. (London), BA (Bristol)

Unwin Education Books: 19
Series Editor: Ivor Morrish

Concepts in Primary Education

JOHN E. SADLER
M.A., Ph.D.

London
GEORGE ALLEN & UNWIN LTD
RUSKIN HOUSE   MUSEUM STREET

© George Allen & Unwin Ltd, 1974

ISBN 0 04 370054 3 hardback
      0 04 370055 1 paperback

Printed in Great Britain
in 10pt Times Roman
by Cox & Wyman Ltd,
London, Fakenham and Reading

Contents

Introduction

During this century there has been a 'teaching revolution' in England and particularly in primary schools. Specific innovations have been made such as the Initial Teaching Alphabet and the Nuffield Projects in mathematics, science and French. Buildings and equipment have been greatly changed towards a more flexible and open-plan design. Mass media have been widely introduced. There have been organisational changes such as team teaching, family grouping and the introduction of integrated timetables. Nevertheless, these modifications are not so important as the drastic and widespread change of approach and attitude towards what is known as the 'child-centred method'. At the beginning of the century the typical primary school had its pupils sitting in fixed rows facing the teacher, taught according to a rigid timetable and syllabus and kept in order by strict discipline. They came to school to learn the basic skills of literacy and only in the infant departments was there any concession to informal learning.

Whether the children of those days were happy or not depended upon how successfully they coped with these basic skills. If the teacher mixed kindness with his firmness and if the home background was encouraging, the situation was tolerable. Teacher and child understood the purpose of the system, which was that the teacher should cover his syllabus by well-prepared lessons and that the child should listen with attention and follow instructions. In so far as more creative activities were allowed, such as art, they were regarded as relaxations but still conformable to conventional standards set by the teacher. If the child could not learn very successfully, through lack of ability or cultural inheritance, or if the teacher could not teach because of inefficiency or petty tyranny, then school was not a happy place.

To this, the typical school of today is a great contrast. Normally the children sit round tables in small groups. They are allowed to talk together and even move around the room or outside it if necessary. They are seldom required to do the same work as each other or to finish at a set time. They have scope for individual choice and are expected to use initiative. Occasionally the teacher may give set lessons or instruct the class as a whole, but this is the exception. For most of the time he is dealing with individuals or groups. He may have a syllabus but does not adhere to it punctiliously. His timetable is determined by such things as the use of the hall or playground or the occurrence of radio programmes. He tries to keep a balance between the various aspects of the curriculum in accordance with school policy but is not greatly concerned about traditional subject boundaries. His discipline is relaxed and permissive and the atmosphere of the class is free and informal. Only in rare cases does he resort to corporal punishment. There is not a drastic change of régime between the infant and junior departments.

It would seem that primary school children are happy; they do not come 'like snails' to school. There is a problem of truancy in some city areas but this is rarely the result of fear or hatred of school. Those who come from middle-class homes tend to flourish when they are given freedom to find things out for themselves, and the modern movement against streaming and 11-plus selection reduces the tension for the slow learners. For the teachers also the situation is favourable because it is more relaxed and intimate personal relationships can be built up. Teachers have lost their dread of HMIs and tend to be less upset by criticism from those in authority.

The new methods are not always successful. For many children from deprived homes the chief attraction of school is that it is warm and colourful, but they are at a disadvantage when given freedom of choice or allowed to discover things for themselves. They are ill-prepared for freedom and become bored by the activities provided for them. In particular, they are not conditioned to regard books as valuable source material. In many cases they have no motivation towards standards of accuracy. They are inclined to believe that copying from books is an acceptable alternative to first-hand discovery. Nor do all teachers feel satisfied with informal methods, which often leave them uncertain about their objectives. They are fearful that to give children freedom of choice when they cannot profit by it may result in disorder. Rather than face chaos they will return to the methods by which they themselves were taught. It has to be admitted that a number of primary teachers give lip-service to an informal approach but are not convinced in their hearts of its value. Then when things go wrong they lose heart and with it the sense of adventure with which they started their careers.

Perhaps it is true that teachers are more conservative than they profess to be and accept changes only superficially. Partly this resistance to innovation is tied up with their fear of losing status or of not knowing what is their social role. Organisational changes such as team teaching or integrated day, may come to teachers psychologically not ready to accept them except at a surface level. The assumption that three or four years of pre-service training is sufficient to give the flexibility of mind necessary to implement worthwhile innovations is untenable, and, for this reason, the *James Report* recommends a considerable expansion of in-service training which it calls the 'third cycle' to 'extend and deepen knowledge of teaching methods and of educational theory' (Chapter 2, paragraph 7).

How far such in-service training will change negative attitudes will depend on the forms it may take. It may not be enough for teachers to attend courses at centres, nor for projects to be planned and initiated by central bodies such as the Schools Council. The teachers themselves must be involved at every step. They must be supported rather than directed, and encouraged to use their initiative rather than to imitate the latest fashion.

This book represents a modest attempt to survey the key concepts which underlie the 'teaching revolution' which has taken place, to examine the arguments and counter-arguments which can be put forward, and to try to strike a reasonable balance between the traditional and the new. Above all it is an attempt to make practical suggestions for putting ideas to the test of experience, and to establish a reasonable foundation for consolidation and further evolution.

NOTE

1 Throughout this book the masculine form of the personal pronoun is used although the majority of primary teachers are feminine. The convention has been dropped only in the case of infant teachers who are normally women, although, happily, a number of men are opting for this work and they will increase with the introduction of 'first' schools.

2 The word 'primary' education is used in its present legal sense as being for children 'who have not attained the age of twelve years and excluding the education of children who have not attained the age of five years (section 114 and section 8, subsection 4, of the Education Act 1944). Reference will be made specifically to nursery schools and to first and middle schools.

Chapter 1

Education

THE RELEVANCE OF A CONCEPT OF EDUCATION

Much that is written about the concept of education is irrelevant to
the day to day work of a primary teacher. Words lose their potency
with repetition and, according to one commentator, show 'signs of
becoming geriatric'.[1] *The Plowden Report* supports the view that
discussion about the aims of education is often too vague to be
helpful by saying that 'high-sounding phrases about the whole child
and his potential development' have 'only a tenuous relationship
with educational practice'. However, this criticism of 'expressions of
benevolent aspiration' and of the 'free and indiscriminate use
of words such as discovery' must be set against the recommendation that 'what is immediately needed is that teachers should
bring to bear on their day to day problems astringent intellectual
scrutiny'.[2]

Nevertheless, the *Plowden Report* tends to fall into the trap which
it condemns. It frequently makes statements based on assumptions
of long-term aims which are not defended. It professes always 'to
start from the nature of the child' and argues that knowledge 'does
not fall into neatly separate compartments'.[3] Throughout, it assumes
that if the child is allowed to express his 'self' freely the long-term
aims will be achieved and the short-term objectives will be satisfied.
Unfortunately, vagueness in both cases blurs the sense of purpose
especially when, as in primary education, external examination
requirements are loosened.

The problem about the 'astringent scrutiny' recommended is that
abstract definitions admit of so many interpretations that their
value is reduced. To define education as involving 'the initiation of
others into worthwhile activities'[4] leaves open the problem of
defining worthwhile. To define education as arising from children's
needs as is done in the Report called *Primary Education in Scotland*
(1965), is even more to invite criticism because it raises the problem

[1] Richmond, Kenneth, *The School Curriculum* (Methuen, 1971), p. 251.
[2] *Plowden Report*, 1967, paras 497 and 550.
[3] *Ibid.*, paras 9 and 505.
[4] Peters, R. S., *Ethics and Education* (Allen & Unwin, 1966), p. 144.

of which needs should be given priority. To say that it is the process by which potentialities are realised raises similar difficulties, since children have many potentialities some of which may be harmful and which should, therefore, be discouraged. Anatole France's definition of education as 'only the art of awakening the natural curiosity of young minds for the purpose of satisfying it afterwards' presupposes that the teacher knows in which direction to guide such natural curiosity. What teachers want is a statement of long-term aims which can be satisfactorily broken down into short-term objectives. Such a statement seems impossible to find.

Is there any way out of the dilemma? We suggest that the question be approached more obliquely but more concretely by considering what kind of person is most likely to make a good teacher and what kind of pupil is likely to be a good end-product. To clarify definitions of the persons concerned will be the best way of defining the process in which they are involved, bearing in mind all the time the infinite variety of both teachers and children. Since the autonomy of persons is the over-arching aim, diversity and uniqueness must be the dominating themes within the common pattern. Educational situations differ so widely that standardisation of either teachers or pupils is either impossible or undesirable but, nevertheless, there must be some common factors.

The first that comes to mind is that the teacher must himself be a learner. Essential to success in teaching is a persistence in the teacher himself of the natural curiosity posited by Anatole France, a continued readiness to admit ignorance coupled with a desire to remedy it, and a life-long enthusiasm for new fields of knowledge and skill to be explored. Versatility is more necessary for a primary teacher than specialisation, not simply because class teaching is the accepted norm, but also because the danger of emphasising the specialist role is that discovery by the pupil may be inhibited.

The two models of teaching may be illustrated diagrammatically thus:

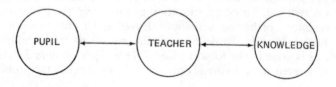

Figure 1   The model in which the pupil comes to knowledge through the teacher's authority

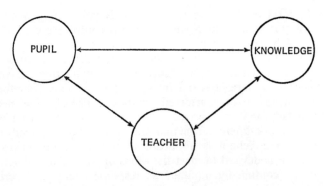

Figure 2 The model in which the pupil comes to knowledge partly through his own initiative and partly with the guidance of the teacher

The important point about the second model is that it suggests that the teacher as well as the pupil is acquiring new knowledge.

However, it is not enough that the teacher should be himself a good learner. He might then be a recluse. He must also have a well-developed capacity for making contact with others, for forming personal relationships, and for acting as a catalyst in the process of acquiring knowledge and skill. In both models there is need for mutual trust and respect, but this is particularly necessary where the teacher deliberately 'stands aside' and adopts a consultative rather than a directive role. This 'standing aside' must be accompanied by sufficient extroversion to make his presence felt; the good teacher is always a 'presence', influencing others without imposing sanctions. Yet extroversion can easily lead the over-confident teacher into too dominating a position in which he loses the capacity to listen to his pupils. So a high degree of sensitivity to those in the subordinate position is another essential characteristic.

Neither enthusiasm nor sensitivity will, however, suffice unless there is also a capacity for organising the learning situation. It has been said that teaching, like genius, depends upon an infinite capacity for taking pains to stimulate learning. A good learning programme involves the effective arrangement of what is to be learnt especially when, as in modern primary education, the emphasis is on giving freedom to the child to learn for himself. To accept the view that education must be child-centred does not imply that it can be left to nature. Just as an unfavourable environment can impede natural development, so a favourable one can accelerate it. Therefore planning the environment is not inconsistent with giving freedom to the learner; rather it is the means by which that freedom can be made effective. John Dewey makes this point categorically, 'The only way in which adults can consciously control the kind of education which the immature can get, is by controlling the environment in which they act, and hence think and feel'.[5] Organisation of the environment has a remedial function in counteracting unfavourable influences and a positive one in stimulating learning. Therefore each situation has to be considered separately. The planning necessary for maladjusted or deprived children or for those from another culture will be different from that suitable for children already favourably placed. School is an artificial, not a natural, environment because it is devised to meet the needs of particular children and it must be continually modified as response changes. Experimental programmes are specially necessary for disadvantaged children either by individual teachers or in large-scale programmes such as the Head Start and Follow Through movements.[6]

A side-effect of good organisation is the well-ordered class, and to many teachers this will appear the prime purpose. Not that it will solve all problems of discipline although it will go far towards minimising them. Open rebellion against authority is mercifully rare in the primary school and the chief cause of trouble is sheer boredom. If each child knows that the teacher is aware of what he is doing and is interested in his point of view, the need for punishments or threats should be greatly reduced. Normally the child wants the approval of the teacher, but even so he may well need the occasional rebuke when he steps over the bounds of good manners and consideration for others.

WHAT DOES TO BE 'EDUCATED' MEAN?

A good answer to this question would necessarily influence the objectives which might be set for the process of education and would, therefore, throw light on the concept of education itself. If, for instance, we gave the answer of the Renaissance humanists it would follow that educated men are an élite: the man 'of lofty nature, moral worth and fame' praised by Vergerius;[7] the 'perfect Governour' of Sir Thomas Elyot;[8] or the man of affairs described by Milton as 'magnanimous in all the arts of peace and war'.[9] But we need not fly so high. To say that an educated man is one who has had a higher

[5] Dewey, John, *Democracy and Education* (Free Press Edn, 1966), p. 18.

[6] Maccoby, Eleanor and Zellner, Miriam, *Experiment in Primary Education, Aspects of Project 'Follow through'* (Harcourt, Brace, 1970).

[7] Quoted from Woodward, W. H., *Vittorino da Feltre and Other Humanist Educators* (CUP, 1897), p. 102.

[8] Elyot, Thomas, *The Boke named the Governour* (Everyman Ed, 1907).

[9] Milton, John, *Tractate on Education* (1644).

or professional training, or even one who has gained public examination successes, would cut out the majority of citizens and would imply that education is a minority privilege. However wide the 'ladder of opportunity' might be, most people would fail to get a footing on it. A system of universal education can only be justified on the grounds that education is a universal potentiality because all children are human and are capable of becoming more fully human. In this sense the brightest and the dullest, the most privileged and the least, are amenable to the educative process and there can be no barriers based on sex, race or class.

Obviously there are infinite degrees but all are capable of some degree of education, and this applies whatever may be the point of emphasis. A. N. Whitehead, for instance, defines education as 'the acquisition of the art of the utilisation of knowledge'.[10] Does not the motor mechanic or the mother of a family acquire this art? Paul Hirst speaks in favour of rationality as the essence of human excellence, but decides that such excellence is only possible 'for someone who has reached a certain level of cognitive development'.[11] But, as he admits, the notion of an 'end-state', when applied to human development, is a problematic one, and rationality is seldom a fixed characteristic. The *Plowden Report* says, 'One obvious purpose of education is to fit children for the society into which they will grow up' so that they will become 'well-balanced with neither emotions nor intellect giving ground to each other'.[12] This sounds fine, but since no one outside a mental hospital is completely lacking in this balance or outside a prison completely unfit for the society in which he lives, the definition is too all-inclusive. The *Newsom Report* avowedly sets out to give a definition of education applicable to the average and below average child and comes to this conclusion, 'All boys and girls need to develop, as well as skills, capacities for thought, judgement, enjoyment and curiosity. They need to develop a sense of responsibility for their work and towards other people, and to begin to arrive at some code of moral and social behaviour which is self-imposed'.[13] The words 'begin to arrive' aptly express the relativity of the concept. Pious platitudes about what the child might hopefully become in an indeterminate future give the teacher little guidance for the present, but provide him with an excuse for doing nothing.

Therefore, instead of considering what it might mean in twenty years' time to be educated, let us consider what kind of behaviour would characterise an educated person, whether child or man. The

[10] Whitehead, A. N., *Aims of Education* (Free Press, 1967), p. 4.
[11] Hirst, Paul, see 'Further Reading' section, p. 54.
[12] *Plowden Report*, 1967, para. 494.
[13] *Newsom Report*, 1963, para 76.

state of being educated is a functional condition, not a substantial one. We cannot define it as an 'essence' or as a faculty or disposition. We can only perceive it in action, in work, in conduct, in such ways as the following:

> Following a purpose with consistency
> Giving reasons for what it is proposed to do
> Tackling a problem with understanding
> Collecting evidence
> Displaying feelings such as bravery, modesty,
>   generosity, sincerity and so on
> Acting in an unselfish way

This list could be extended indefinitely because there is a consensus of opinion as to what kind of conduct is meant by rationality, moral virtue, emotional sensitivity, balance and strength of purpose, and a general recognition that these desirable activities occur in infinite degrees of consistency and strength. This is what it means to be educated—a state of affairs which can occur in the youngest child even though at a low level. Then the process of education means creating the conditions in which children will demonstrate their state of being educated in the present, not their potentiality for the future.

THE SUBJECT OF EDUCATION

The question of aims and objectives is an important part of the concept of education but there are other aspects which call for consideration. We need to analyse the process itself in terms of the theoretical principles which underlie it, i.e. to treat it as a subject in its own right. Thus the practice of medicine is based upon a science of the functioning of the human body, and the practice of civil engineering upon the relevant science of structures and forces. It is tempting to think that the practice of education will similarly come to be based on scientific theories about human learning and behaviour. That this is possible is the view of a number of people, of whom B. F. Skinner may be taken as representative. Skinner's argument is that there is sufficient uniformity in human behaviour to give rise to 'laws' which have as much validity as those which govern medicine or engineering. The science of human behaviour, which Skinner proposes, would arise from the study of external behaviour. He would agree that the human being is very complex and that his behaviour is often unpredictable, but this is because all the relevant facts are not available to us. Skinner concentrates his attention upon that particular aspect of human behaviour which seems most amenable to scientific study, namely the stimulus–response situation. His claim is that by doing this we could remove most of the uncertainty and vagueness about the educational process. From this simple psychological basis, he would construct a logical programme of learning so that any child could learn surely and easily. He holds that the real problem of education is one of mechanising the process, either through a living teacher or a machine, it does not matter which, so that we can teach 'rapidly, thoroughly and expeditiously a large part of what we now teach slowly, incompletely and with wasted effort'. Skinner assumes that we know intuitively what we are aiming for; we should direct our attention to the kinds of reinforcement necessary to bring it about.

The proposal to reduce the concept of education to psychological theory made some headway because it was widely felt that the amorphous body of so-called principles of education was a very inadequate basis for the practice of teaching. However, it was soon realised that other issues were involved: sociological, historical and philosophical issues. Thus the present subject of 'education' developed with its supporting disciplines, some of them still struggling for recognition, but all of them determined to be academically respectable in terms of the intellectual rigour recommended by the *Plowden Report*. The *James Report* takes the matter a stage further, by suggesting that the present division between 'main subjects' and 'education' should be overcome by including in the 'special' studies some which are obviously relevant to teaching, such as child development, and including them also in the 'general' studies, but that the more rigorous study of the concept of education should be deferred until sufficient experience had been gained in the second and third 'cycles' of training to make it meaningful.[14]

The efforts which have been made over the past ten years and the proposals now being put forward should go a long way to making education a subject capable of stretching the minds of the most able students, and also capable of making a substantial contribution to radical change in our system of universal education. The supporting disciplines of psychology, sociology and philosophy have now been joined by a subject generally called 'curriculum studies' in which the context, design and development of what is done in schools is brought under examination. This may offset the tendency which had crept in for advanced studies to be too far removed from children and schools. In a number of colleges this subject has now been raised to the same status as main subjects and education with the great advantage that all the staff have been involved in it. Curriculum studies have, therefore, become something of a bridge between

[14] *James Report*, 1972, Chapter 4, para. 13.

departments and have also provided a link between theoretical studies and the practice of teaching. It has been shown that standards can be achieved in studies where the practical side is emphasised equal to those achieved in more academic subjects.

The number of students going on to take a B.Ed. degree at the end of four years is increasing. The Open University has provided a means by which many practising teachers can study education at a deeper level in their spare time. If the proposals of the *James Report* are implemented teaching will eventually become an all-graduate profession and it will be the rule for practising teachers to be given ample opportunity for in-service training. At the same time, there is growing awareness of the danger that theory and practice will be divorced, and the recommendation of the *James Report* is that teachers should take more responsibility than hitherto for training, and that a substantial part of the training course should be school-based. The opinion is widely held that not enough research is being done in education as compared with other areas of knowledge. There may be truth in this, but the problem is to find topics for research which teachers will find relevant to their situation. In too many cases research seems to be undertaken as an end in itself and not because some problem demands investigation.

The great problem is of co-ordination between the specialisms that have developed in the education course; between main subjects and education; between theoretical studies and practical teaching; and, above all, between colleges and schools. It is accentuated by the present drive towards larger colleges and larger schools. Yet there are frequent complaints of the time-consuming nature of co-ordinating committees and meetings. The need for taking stock of the concept of education is, however, obvious to all concerned: tutors, teachers and students.

One problem which calls for attention is how far the scientific character of educational studies can, or should, be maintained. It is tempting to think that by the application of science we could teach a child to understand a mathematical concept with as much assurance as we could treat him for a physical illness. The demand that research should generally be empirical is an expression of this longing for relative certitude, and of a belief that in the fullness of time education should be as exact a science, as, say, biology or even physics. Everyone knows that science, even physics, cannot predict with absolute precision; the trouble with education is that it seems to have no precision at all. But should not this be a matter for congratulation rather than despair? The essential fact about human beings which makes them unique in the world of nature is their infinite flexibility. If we could envisage a science of behaviour so exact that it could determine the end-product it would give us only a nightmare. It is true that man must understand his own nature even though his purpose is frequently to circumvent it; and this fact is specially important to those dealing with human beings. A few illustrations relevant to the primary school may make this point.

B. F. Skinner did not think that the application of scientific laws to human development would destroy human personality. On the contrary, the Utopian society which he foresaw was anything but moronic. However it is unlikely that human beings would ever submit to the methods of conditioning successful with pigeons. In some ways pigeons are more amenable to training than children; they respond predictably. But the ability to respond predictably does *not* imply the ability to think, and that is the difference. Children can be made to give the right answers to questions without understanding what is at stake in the question. But they are not born with understanding and the length of time which this ability takes to develop is both a strength and a weakness. Jean Piaget has made a remarkable impact on the thinking of teachers by his insistence that the development of thought, in all its aspects, has a biological basis. Until a child has gone through 'stages' in which he only thinks through 'concrete operations' with his hands, feet and body he cannot think with 'logical operations' in his mind. First the action, then, after it has been mentally digested for a considerable time, the thought. Thought is, in fact, action instilled into the mind. This empirical fact puts serious limitations on the effectiveness of programmed learning for children. It may be that for certain limited skills a series of logical steps can be devised which will have the great advantage of allowing each child to proceed at his own pace, but conceptual development cannot be accelerated by a logical programme when the child is still incapable of logical thinking. Thus Skinner came to his conclusions about education by a scientific study of animal behaviour, but Piaget refuted these conclusions by his scientific study of children. He defines the limits within which programmed learning can be effective.

But Piaget's own conclusions must not be too readily accepted, and they do not, or should not, imply that we must always wait for biological maturation. His stages are signposts but no more. This was dramatically demonstrated in 1971 at the meeting of the British Association when Peter Bryant claimed that he could bring even four-year-olds to understand abstract concepts. The argument against this is that to train children to give the 'right' answers is not to give them understanding, but this only goes to prove that the 'wrong' answers given by Piaget's children do not prove that they had *no* understanding. Understanding is relative and though it does take time to develop, the stages are not as discrete as Piaget seems to suggest. Certainly it is true that understanding and language development go closely together, and this fact has given the Russian psychologists, Luria and Vygotsky, sufficient warrant to suggest a programme of linguistic experience which might greatly accelerate conceptual development. That this acceleration is more effective if applied at an early age gives a psychological as well as a social reason for the increase in nursery education proposed by the Government White Paper of 1972, *Education: A Framework for Expansion*. Thus science is constantly being used to circumvent science; a general law is discovered so that its effects can be controlled. Nevertheless, whenever personal relationships are involved it is their quality which is a determining factor in how the situation develops. For instance, in the case of the teaching of reading there are several methods each of which could claim to be the most effective on empirical evidence, but the most recent literature shows that whichever method is used the most important factor is the teacher and his relationship with the child.[15]

The concept of education always involves two factors—the personal and the social—which must be kept in balance. This involves constant interaction between the psychological and the sociological approach. Psychology is concerned with the behaviour and mental process of the individual upon which biological and social forces act, while sociology is concerned with the structure and functioning of social groups and their effects upon individuals. These two are, however, parts of the same process.

Take, for instance, the question of achievement in school work. From a psychological point of view the variation between one child and another can be accounted for in terms of intelligence. If a child's performance is well below his IQ level it is concluded that he is under-achieving, and vice versa. But within recent years a great deal of research has gone to show that social class is also an important factor and that the socio-cultural background of a child can depress or raise his level of educational performance. Both these conclusions are based on empirical evidence and might lead one to suppose that they were fixed by nature. It is realised, however, that neither IQ nor social class is fixed. Suitable training and environment can alter innate intelligence, and similarly, suitable training and environment can influence social class. The fact that change can be brought about more easily the younger the child is, simply points to the importance of primary education.

The optimistic view of education is that it can bring about change in the individual and in society. The danger of this view is that it

[15] Southgate V., and Roberts G. R., *Reading: Which Approach?* (ULP, 1970).

implies that the intention of the teacher is the important factor rather than the intention of the child, which is contrary to the child-centred view which accepts the infinite variety of human beings and seeks to guide each one to educate himself. The 'humanness' which is the goal of the process is many-sided and too much of an attempt at manipulation may be self-defeating. The teacher may guide but should not direct, even covertly. The hidden persuader is as much an enemy of individuality as the open tyrant.

We come, therefore, to the view that education is essentially a two-way process in which teacher and learner benefit and influence each other; perhaps the nearest analogy is that of free conversation where there is the ebb and flow of opinion and each side stimulates the other. This concept is aptly expressed in the following quotation:

'Education, properly speaking, is an initiation into the skill and partnership of this conversation in which we learn to recognise the voices, to distinguish the proper occasions of utterance, and in which we acquire the intellectual and moral habits appropriate to conversation. And it is this conversation which, in the end, gives place and character to every human activity and utterance'[16]

The problem for the teacher is how to make this dialogue relevant and meaningful to the child. There is a barrier to communication between the world of the adult and that of the child which must be overcome by an effort from both sides. For the adult, the effort necessary is to appreciate and to some extent understand the intuitive experiences of childhood expressed in dramas and mysteries, and this demands from him a considerable effort of sympathy and imagination. Intuition is not only fruitful; it is absolutely necessary for any entry into the adult world of the analysis of problems. J. S. Bruner has discussed this problem in his book *The Relevance of Education*, in which he says 'the aim of a balanced schooling is to enable the child to proceed intuitively when necessary and to analyse when appropriate'; he goes on, 'Unexploited intuition that goes nowhere and does not deepen itself by further digging into the material is somehow not sufficient to bring the person to the full use of his capacities. Intuition is an invitation to go further—whether intuitively or analytically. And it is with the training of people to go further in this way that we are concerned'.[17]

The child, on his side, also has to make an effort of the imagination. He finds it difficult to appreciate the relevance of what the adult tries to bring before him. It is not enough that the adult should try to relate knowledge of the child's own experience by raising problems

[16] Oakeshott, Michael, *Rationalism in Politics and other Essays* (Methuen, 1962), p. 199.
[17] Bruner, J. S., see 'Further Reading', pp. 83 and 88.

about the home or the neighbourhood which, to the child, are just not meaningful. To quote Bruner again, 'Adults often fail to recognise the task of conversion necessary to give their questions some intrinsic significance for the child . . . Children are not often predisposed to, or skilful in, problem finding or in recognising the hidden conjectural features in the tasks set for them . . . children in school spend extraordinary effort and time in figuring out what it is that the teacher wants'.[18]

How can this conversion be brought about and what objectives should teachers set for themselves in the process? If we could find convincing answers to these questions we should be well on the way to defining education itself. If it is true, as Bruner asserts, that children do not see the relevance of the kind of questions teachers are apt to ask, we conclude that what is necessary is that children should frame their own problems. We must exploit their intuitive searching towards problem finding. This was, in fact, the leading principle put forward in the *Nuffield Junior Science Project*, and it was the principle which teachers found hardest to accept. It was based on the assumption that all children will, if encouraged, ask their own questions which, although they may not seem particularly worthwhile to the teacher, will give them a starting point for inquiry. Here again we might refer to Bruner's dictum, 'If we want to look ahead to what is special about a school we should ask how to train generations to *find* problems, to look for them.[19] The argument is that 'good' problems are the chief vehicles for a 'good' curriculum but the goodness arises from the fact that they develop intuitively in the child's own mind. The teacher's function is to foster the process. Bruner suggests several ways in which this function can be exercised. One is to encourage the child to explore contrasts because this helps the child to organise his knowledge in ways that help discovery in particular situations: 'Readiness to explore contrasts provides a choice among the alternatives that might be relevant.'[20] Another is to help the child to gain competence rather than particular performance. We should not aim to teach the child 'about' this or that area of adult knowledge so much as to help him to 'know how' to operate in it. Once he has gained a minimum of this competence the relevance of problems involved in it will come to him. The third way is to make use of the 'dramas and mysteries' which are so basic to the child's mental experience. Essentially, education is a question of relevance, though relevance is always a matter of degree. In a sense, all things are relevant to each other but we see a closer connection between some than others. Obviously, what is relevant to a child is not the same as what is relevant to an adult, just as no two adults see relevance in exactly the same way. But relevance, even the most apparently far-fetched, is always worth exploring to see where it leads. This, then, gives us a clue as to the nature of the dialogue which goes on between teacher and pupil.

FURTHER READING

Archambault, R. D., *Philosophical Analysis and Education*, (Routledge & Kegan Paul, 1965).

Bantock, G. H., *The Implications of Literacy* (Univ. of Leicester, 1966).

Brearley, Molly, *Fundamentals in the First School*. (Blackwell, 1970).

Bruner, J. S., *The Relevance of Education* (Allen & Unwin, 1972).

Chazan, Maurice, *Compensatory Education* (Butterworth, 1973).

Cohen, Brenda, *Educational Thought: An Introduction* (Macmillan, 1969).

Dearden, R. F., *The Philosophy of Primary Education* (Routledge & Kegan Paul, 1968).

Gagné, R. M., *The Conditions of Learning* (Holt, Rinehart, 1965).

Harris, Alan, *Thinking about Education* (Heinemann, 1970).

Hirst, P. H. and Peters, R. S., *The Logic of Education* (Routledge & Kegan Paul, 1970).

Peters, R. S. (ed.), *The Concept of Education* (Routledge & Kegan Paul, 1967).

Peters, R. S., *Ethics and Education* (Allen & Unwin, 1966).

Reid, L. A., *Philosophy and Education* (Heinemann, 1962).

Tibble, J. W. (ed), *The Study of Education* (Routledge & Kegan Paul, 1966).

Chapter 2

Training

The relationship between education and training is a close one; it would be impossible to conceive any form of education which did not include an element of training, though there may be forms of training in which education is minimal such as the training of circus animals or the 'square-bashing' once thought to be essential for military purposes. Even in such cases it is wrong to be dogmatic. Seals, for instance, show a highly intelligent response to their training, which might be considered relevant to education. As far as humans are concerned it is hard to think of any form of training, however mechanical, which does not include some educational element. The broad distinction is that training is concerned with competence in performing while education is concerned with giving thought and attention. In some activities there is both a low level of competence and a low level of understanding, as in some factory operations; while in others there is a high level of both, as in brain surgery. The two elements will be in different proportions in different activities. Thus, in the building industry, both the bricklayer and the civil engineer have a skill which comes from training but more understanding is involved in the work of the engineer. In many cases the distinction between the two elements cannot be sharply distinguished because they will vary according to the individual, the situation, and the level of performance required. Thus, the most difficult kind of skill, such as flying an aeroplane, may from time to time slip into mechanical procedure while the simplest kind, such as knitting, may, on occasion, involve self-striving for style.

Thus the relationship is one of emphasis and degree and it may be looked at from various points of view. One is that education is concerned with long-term aims, and training with short-term objectives. Thus the education of a milkman would be concerned with customer relationships, the processes of marketing and the possible sources of contamination; while his training would be concerned with competence in driving a truck, in handling the milk bottles and in keeping customers' accounts. Whether punctuality and courtesy would count as education or training would depend on how they were dealt with. Another example would be that of military education and training. An officer would certainly be trained in the use of weapons, but he would also be educated in strategy and tactics; whereas a private soldier would normally be more concerned with training in offensive and defensive techniques. Often the distinction between education and training is indistinct. So, although teachers are trained in the use of audio-visual appliances, it is right that they should be educated to have an understanding of audio-visual perception. Education is based on the theory of learning by insight, but training is more closely related to stimulus-response. Animals can be trained by suitable reinforcement to respond as desired. So can children, but children can also be educated to show insight into what they are doing.

Another way of distinguishing between education and training would be to think of education as involving a change of perspective but of training as being concerned with the performance of specific operations. Thus the educational aim of teaching literature might be to give to the learner an appreciation of verbal expression and a capacity to analyse human nature, while the aim of training might be to give him familiarity with a particular text and an ability to answer questions about it. Education is concerned with giving intrinsic satisfactions such as a love of learning for its own sake or a readiness to investigate a problem to its logical conclusion. Though more rewarding in the long run, these are more difficult for the teacher to pursue or the pupil to accept than are the more assessable satisfactions of training. The learner tends to want precise instruction and demonstration. He likes a model to conform to. While education involves self-criticism and adaptability to varying situations, training is concerned with conformity to standard procedures, automatic responses and regular habits.

In both education and training practice is important, but there is a difference because in education each repetition is made an opportunity to learn some modification or improvement of response. In education, flexibility is the essential quality looked for, in training it is standardisation of technique. Education is more open-ended, it allows for individual variation and is adaptable to different situations. Training, on the other hand, is more reproductive, more conditioned, more stereotyped.

The distinction may be interpreted by reference to two writers who have greatly influenced teachers: Herbart and William James. Herbart argued that the purpose of education was to modify conduct in a desirable way, but that this could only be done indirectly by instruction contained in the ideas presented to the mind of the learner. As the ideas were assimilated they combined to form what Herbart called a 'circle of thought', and this was the basis for the formation of character. Thus he says, 'Instruction (i.e. training) will form the circle of thought, and education the character. The last is nothing without the first. Herein is contained the whole sum of my pedagogy'. William James, in 1892, gave some lectures to teachers which were later published as 'Talks to Teachers'. They were very popular and had great influence on American teachers. One of his main themes was that teachers must train children in as many good habits as possible so that their minds might be free for education. He speaks of making the nervous system the ally, instead of the enemy, of mental development. Thus he says, 'We must make automatic and habitual, as early as possible, as many useful actions as we can, and as carefully guard against the growing into ways that are likely to be disadvantageous. The more of the details of our daily life we can hand over to the effortless custody of automatism, the more our higher powers of mind will be set free for their own proper work'.[1] This book is still worth reading because of its discussion of the relationship between education and training.

For an even fuller discussion of the relationship between the two we might go back to John Amos Comenius, the seventeenth-century Czech educationalist, who was the first to offer to the world the prospect of a universal education so that, as he puts it, 'the whole of the human race may become educated men'. His plea was that schools should become 'forging places of humanity'. At the same time, no one was more convinced than Comenius of the necessity for training. He was almost obsessional about the proper use of time since, as he reckoned there were 2,495 hours per year available for the 'serious work of life', a 'vast stock of learning' could be acquired with a careful organisation of time.[2] Comenius claimed to provide teachers with a 'method of teaching and of learning with such certainty that the desired result must follow'. Without it, he says that the teacher would be like 'an unpractised gardener' who plants trees, and that 'the few that prosper do so rather through chance than through skill'.[3] His favourite analogies for the educative process were printing-presses and clocks. He would have rejected any suggestion that this made the whole process too mechanical because, as he says, children 'being malleable, must be utilized for education'.[4] This view is not consistent with the modern teaching

[1] James, William, *Talks to Teachers* (Longmans Green, 1913), p. 67.
[2] Comenius, J. A., *Great Didactic*, Chapter XIV, 22.
[3] *Ibid.*, Chapter XVI, 3.
[4] Comenius, J. A., *Pampaedia*, Chapter V, 14.

revolution but it does suggest that training and education are polar opposites supplementing each other.

SKILLS OF 'KNOWING HOW'

So far in our examination we have argued that education and training represent two kinds of knowledge—knowledge of systems of thought, of 'knowing that', and knowledge of efficient performance, or 'knowing how'; and it has been implied that the first is superior to the second. It is presumed that intelligent 'know-how' must arise from some previous understanding of what it means. Gilbert Ryle is one who protests against this view. He calls it an 'intellectual legend' and claims that intelligent practice is not a 'step-child of theory'. On the contrary, 'theorising is one practice among others and is itself stupidly or intelligently conducted'.[5] He argues that 'knowing how' to do something is not simply a matter of knowing how to perform it efficiently or successfully; it must also include 'the ability to detect and correct lapses, to repeat and improve upon successes, to profit from the examples of others and so forth'.[6] Thus there are many parallels between 'knowing how' and 'knowing that', as well as certain divergencies. Certain forms of 'knowing how' are so automatic and mechanical that it is hard to find any intelligence factor in them. On the other hand, certain forms of 'knowing that' need not be accompanied by efficient performance. For example, we may believe in a principle without practising it; we may support a statement because there is good evidence for it, or logical grounds for it, without being committed to any action. Thus 'knowing how' has no necessary connection with belief or evidence or truth; it is simply a capacity to perform intelligently as well as efficiently. To 'know how' is to have a skill, but the degree of intelligence involved may vary considerably.

At a low level are many of the habits which have become, in William James' words, 'handed over to the effortless custody of automatism'—walking, for instance. However, we can imagine circumstances in which such automatic habits demand a high degree of intelligence: Gilbert Ryle gives the case of a mountaineer 'walking over ice-covered rocks in a high wind in the dark'.[7] Other instances would be walking a tight-rope or taking part in a walking race. In all these cases a habit, normally automatic, would require care, vigilance and self-criticism. Take, for instance, the learning of multiplication

[5] Ryle, Gilbert, *The Concept of Mind* (Hutchinson, 1949—Penguin Edn.), p. 27.
[6] *Ibid.*, p. 29.
[7] *Ibid.*, p. 42.

tables, which could be at a low level of intelligence, where the child could not say what 8 × 7 came to without reciting the whole of the table, or at higher level where the response would not only be automatic but would include knowledge of other complementary number bonds such as 7 × 8 and 80 × 7. The object of training a habit is not simply to make it automatic but to invest it with more intelligence.

Then we may think of a skill of 'knowing how' as a propensity where the intelligence element is normally higher than in habit; because it implies a tendency to behave in a certain way in circumstances which are similar, but different in some respects. The skill has to be adapted to the particular situation. Take, for instance, the skill of poetry recitation. A child might get into a habit of reciting one particular poem very well, but if presented with another poem of different kind he would find it a new challenge. Gradually, with experience, he would acquire a propensity to tackle any new poem. Each one would be unique but the same skill would be basic to the recitation of all. Propensities are developed by constant practice in different situations, by favourable social conditions and by strong motivation. They imply conscious and critical understanding. For instance, a child might fall into a habit of mis-spelling from which he could only be rescued by forming a counter propensity for paying attention to words.

A technique is a different kind of skill from either a habit or a propensity and implies knowledge of a standardised procedure or routine. It is the correct sequence of movements or operations which is important. Eventually the sequence becomes so automatic that it is habitual but normally it requires more concentration than mere habit. For instance, there is a difference between learning to walk and learning to dive. Walking is part of the normal maturation process of a human being, but diving does not come naturally. To teach diving the correct sequence of body movements has to be shown in slow motion, then they have to be repeated by the learner with varying degrees of success. Eventually a new pattern of movement is formed and we might say that a technique is acquired. The formation of techniques is important in an industrialised society where technology has put at our disposal a wide range of machines and gadgets for cooking, washing, cleaning, gardening and so on, each of which has its appropriate technique. Understanding of these gadgets frequently depends upon the printed instructions supplied and skill in dealing with this kind of literature must have an increasing importance in the education of children. To acquire this skill it is not necessary to have at our disposal understanding of all the machinery of modern life, because almost any operation can be reduced to a technique and taught accordingly.

Gilbert Ryle gives as an example of intelligent 'knowing how' the playing of chess, and certainly here the intelligence factor seems more pronounced than in habit, propensity or technique. We could describe it as a facility. After the appropriate habits have been formed, for instance of the knight's move, and a propensity has been gained for various tactical movements of attack or defence, and techniques such as castling have been mastered, there still remains the necessity for a facility for checkmating strategies. Young players often find this the most difficult skill to acquire. They concentrate on the next move but fail to plan a sequence of moves or fail to perceive and fail to counteract the sequence which their opponent is planning. Teachers should think of as many skills as possible which involve this kind of facility and which are a challenge to the intelligence of young children.

Is there a kind of skill which does not involve performance at all, or only minimally? Critical appreciation is such a skill. Of course it is helped if efficient performance is also present, but this is not necessary. For instance, a crippled child might still have a well-developed appreciation of excellence in football. Here the skill is that of being able to judge performance rather than to carry it out. Can one be a good musical judge without being able to play an instrument or perform as a vocalist? It would certainly be difficult, but a love of music, experience of the fellowship of musicians and a knowledge of musical theory might make a person a good judge of the performance of others; especially if, in addition, he had sufficient flexibility to be able to appreciate new forms and innovations. This kind of skill is important in primary education because the ability to judge performance beyond present capacity is a source of motivation for later effort.

THE SKILLS OF PRIMARY TEACHING

In the traditional school the skills necessary for success were fairly specific. The good primary teacher had all the habits, propensities, techniques and facilities necessary for planning and giving 'good' lessons, i.e. lessons which followed a logical sequence, which were carefully timed and which had suitable introductions and conclusions. Each lesson had a structure, but in its delivery the teacher had to be able to engage and hold the attention of the class by appropriate techniques of maintaining order, by questioning and by effective exposition. Among the means at his disposal the teacher had various incentives such as marks, privileges, status symbols or teacher approval; and various disincentives such as denial of marks, privileges or status symbols or the sanctions of rebuke, unpleasant tasks and, in the last resort, punishments. The good disciplinarian was one whose authority was so assured that he could maintain order with a minimum of incentives or disincentives. His authority was based partly on respect for him as a person, partly on eternal vigilance but partly on bluff. Whether he was a benevolent despot or a petty tyrant was not so important as the overriding condition that he should be able to keep order by giving the class so much to do that idleness was impossible—so many sums to be finished, so many exercises to be completed, so many tasks to be accomplished by a fixed time. The panacea for classroom disorder was well-filled time.

These traditional skills of exposition, discipline and work organisation are still important, but the teaching revolution has changed the emphasis to other skills and the atmosphere in all schools is no longer conducive to the old pattern. Children are not so easily overawed. Public opinion is not so favourable to punishment. The teacher-stereotype is different. The atmosphere is more relaxed. So skills other than the old ones have to be cultivated. Conditions, too, have changed so as to reduce the necessity for exposition, discipline and work organisation. There are still classes of over forty, old buildings and cramped rooms but they are the exception not the rule. Other changes may be mentioned: a majority of women teachers being married and having families, a much wider and more attractive range of books, and the introduction of technical aids. School situations are less uniform than they used to be and this calls for a variety of skills suitable for the two-teacher village school, the council estate school, the immigrant school or the middle-class suburban school. A teacher who excels in one type might be unsuccessful in another.

Professional attitudes have changed too. Traditionally, the primary teacher had full responsibility for the whole curriculum of his class. Within his own four walls he was master of the situation and either feared or resented interference. His attitude to his pupils was paternalistic, possibly possessive, and he gained his professional satisfaction from watching and assisting the development, both moral and scholastic, of his charges. There are still many teachers who follow this pattern but the teaching revolution has brought in people with different attitudes about their role and status. This new type of teacher is more inclined to specialise if he is thinking of the middle school situation; if he is more drawn to the younger children it is probably because he is orientated towards the infants school ethos which ignores subject and curriculum boundaries. Women are always likely to be more drawn in this direction than men, but their attitudes have changed too. They see themselves as being in charge of an extended family and bring to their work many of the feminine skills of the good mother. Various developments such as open-plan buildings and team teaching make modern teachers, whether male or female, more ready to take a wider view of their responsibilities to include factors other than those arising from their own class; more ready to welcome other adults into the classroom; and more likely to develop contacts with the outside world.

The old skills are still important but they take on different forms. Take, for instance, exposition. The modern teacher does not often give set lessons of thirty minutes or longer. If he does address the class as a whole it is for much shorter periods; his exposition is more likely to arise incidentally from someone's question or as part of a genuine discussion. The set lesson is no longer necessary but the power of clear speech and lucid explanation is just as important. Then there is the skill of leadership which, under former conditions, consisted of keeping order and maintaining authority. The teacher still has to project his personality but he does it in less obvious ways. One can go into a classroom where the teacher is hidden from view because he is sitting with an individual child, but the children are in some subtle way well aware of his presence and he gives each of them the feeling of being under surveillance. Leadership is more a question of group dynamics than of asserting authority from the front of the class. The old sanctions have lost much of their force and the teacher of today must win consent not impose it. Fortunately junior children are seldom consciously in revolt and they bear no malice, but they are easily discouraged and thrive on praise. The organisation of work is just as important as ever but it takes more individualised forms. The textbook is less in evidence, being replaced by work cards, but these are only better if they are more adapted to the particular children using them. Work still has to be checked and marked but more on an individual basis.

There are new skills demanded by the new style of teaching. The old class teacher autonomy is less strong than it was; the greater flexibility of timetable and curriculum has reduced the scope for head-teacher authority; and the likelihood of immobility in one school is less. On the other hand, there is more opportunity for co-operation between colleagues; school government is more democratic; and relations with the outside world are acceptable. These changes put a premium on the skills of working with others in teams, committees or parent–teacher associations. Since the primary teacher is now so little encumbered with syllabus requirements he has both opportunity and duty to create an educative environment. This requires skills of display and presentation in the arranging of visual material or in the organisation of interest-corners. In turn this involves all the techniques of audio-visual presentation: lettering, demonstrating, and illustrating diagrammatically; as well as the manipulation of all the modern mechanical aids such as episcopes, slide-projectors, ciné-projectors, tape-recorders and so on.

THE TRAINING OF A PRIMARY TEACHER

Nothing could better illustrate the change of approach in primary education than the changes which are taking place in the training of primary teachers. The old emphasis on exposition, discipline and organisation was backed up by masters of method, demonstration schools and criticism lessons. It is much harder to give a model of what is wanted today because informality can hardly be demonstrated formally. Assessment of teaching skill is so much more difficult that there have been strong moves to abandon grading altogether. The separation of colleges of education from schools has led to the recommendations of the *James Report* that a kind of apprenticeship system should be introduced, with students spending the whole of their third year attached to a school and supervised by practising teachers. In so far as students are attached to colleges for the rest of their course the shape of teaching practice will be changed so that students work in teams, join teams in the schools or form playgroups for children in the college neighbourhood. This will mean that the method of final assessment of practical teaching will have to take new forms, since the old will not apply.

Nevertheless, there is a strong argument that training should be an important part of the college course. It would be fatal if the college confined itself to main-subject study and the theory of education. This, however, calls for much reform of the professional courses, which have tended to be the Achilles heel of teacher training. Certain points may be put forward as a basis for discussion on what might be an ideal college-based professional course:

1. It must have enhanced prestige and be seen to be taken seriously by the authorities. Unless this is the case the colleges will move towards even greater isolation from schools than at present.

2. The professional courses must, as far as possible, put the students into the same kind of position that their pupils will be in subsequently. That is to say, they must learn the skills of informal teaching by being put into informal learning situations themselves. Thus, the emphasis in subjects like science, geography, and history must be on self-discovery; the students must themselves experience what is entailed in doing an experiment or in making an environmental survey or in setting up an historical museum.

3. The emphasis must be on versatility of skills. It would be desirable, though too much to be expected, that every student should be able to paint, to letter, to type, to play the guitar or some similar instrument, to take part in spontaneous drama, to take and develop photographs, to take part in an archaeological dig and so on. Obviously in the time available there would have to be selection, but this should be made as wide as possible; and the level and number of skills could be extended and developed by subsequent in-service education. As a minimum requirement every student should be trained in the use of all the commonly used audio-visual aids.

4. The principle of learning by doing should be applied in every subject. For instance, in the English course the student should have the experience of constructing his own reading scheme, in the mathematics class he should make number games and apparatus, and in the drama class he should take part in play production.

5. Inevitably there are some parts of a professional course in which the student's own knowledge is being widened, but there the emphasis should be on practical research. For instance, a course on the teaching of immigrant children should stress the materials and sources available. It is much to be desired that every teacher of young children should have practical experience in the varieties of story-telling and reading and be able to make up his own stories suitable for children. In geography, history, science and social studies the emphasis should be on field work rather than book work.

6. The ideal would be that every student should take a practical course in language and mathematics, in audio-visual aids and physical education; and a number of elective courses, the number being dependent on the time and resources available but sufficient to give reasonable versatility.

There are still certain skills common to all subjects, especially those relating to class management, and for these various methods are suggested:

1. The simulation exercise in which students take on typical roles in the classroom situation and test out, and afterwards discuss, possible outcomes. The simulation is a game but it raises fundamental issues for consideration.

2. Micro-teaching in which one particular aspect of a typical teaching situation is practised and then discussed.

3. Team teaching in which a student joins a team of practising teachers, takes part in their discussions and shares the responsibility for organisation.

4. The college-school partnerships in which it becomes accepted practice for teachers to hold seminars in the college, or for students

to go as a group to schools where good teachers are practising and discuss with them their methods and difficulties. The *Plowden Report* puts emphasis on this in the following words: 'partnership between schools and training institutions is the key to satisfactory arrangements for teaching practice and is worth almost any effort to achieve' (paragraph 992).

5. In this matter of partnership the development of teachers' centres all over the country may be noted. College lecturers, local authority advisers, and teachers are sharing in making these available for pre-service and in-service training.

6. An important aspect of in-service training is the participation of teachers in schemes of experimental and curricular innovation initiated by the Schools Council and the National Foundation for Educational Research.

FURTHER READING

Allen, Dwight and Ryan, Kevin, *Micro Teaching* (Addison Wesley, 1969).

Bassett, G. W., *Innovation in Primary Education* (John Wiley, 1970).

Blackie, John, *Inside the Primary School* (HMSO, 1967).

Brearley, Molly, *et. al.*, *Educating Teachers* (Macmillan, 1972).

Bruner, J. S., *Towards a Theory of Instruction* (Harvard Univ. Press, 1966).

Byrnes, R. J., *Primary Teacher Training* (OUP, 1960).

Clegg, Alec, *The Changing Primary School* (Chatto & Windus, 1972).

Close, David, *School Discipline* (Cambridge Aids to Learning, 1972).

Cohen, A. and Garner, N., *A Student's Guide to Teaching Practice* (ULP, 1966).

Davies, Ivor and Hartley, J., *Contributions to an Educational Technology* (Butterworth, 1972).

Duthie, J. H., *Primary School Survey; Study of the Teacher's Day* (HMSO, Scotland, 1970).

Featherstone, Joseph, *British Primary Schools Today* (Macmillan, 1971).

Gardner, D. E. M. and Cass, J. E., *The Role of the Teacher in the Infants and Nursery School* (Pergamon, 1965).

Garnett, Emmeline, *Area Resource Centre* (E. Arnold, 1972).

Hilsum, Sydney, *The Teacher at Work* (NFER, 1972).

Howes, Virgil M., *Individualisation of Instruction: A Teaching Strategy* (Collier Macmillan, 1970).

Jarman, Christopher, *Display and Presentation in the Classroom* (Black, 1972).

Kay, N. C., *Practical Teaching* (Evans, 1971).

Lamb, Brydon, *Educational Technology and Team Teaching* (National Commission for Audio-visual Aids in Education, 1970).

Morris R., *The In-service Education of Teachers* (Exeter Univ. Press., 1966).

Probert, Howard and Jarman, Christopher, *A Junior School* (Macmillan, 1971).

Rogers, Vincent R., *Teaching in British Primary Schools* (Collier Macmillan, 1970).

Stones E. and Morris, S., *Teaching Practice Problems and Perspectives* (Methuen, 1972).

Tansey, Patrick, *Educational Aspects of Simulation* (McGraw-Hill, 1971).

Taylor, John L., *Simulation in the Classroom* (Penguin, 1972).

Turner, Barry, *Discipline in Schools* (Ward Lock, 1973).

White, William F., *Tactics for Teaching the Disadvantaged* (McGraw-Hill, 1971).

Chapter 3

Initiation

MODELS OF TEACHING

In trying to understand the differences and common elements in traditional and modern primary education it is sometimes helpful to look for analogies. Thus we may take a typical example or an apt simile or make a diagrammatic representation. These analogies may be called models because they put in concrete form what is believed to be the essence of a principle—the Garden of Eden, Plato's Cave, Animal Farm and Lord of the Flies may be considered instances of this. The purpose of the model is to get to the heart of the matter. Jesus used his parables for this purpose; and Socrates took his models from the everyday life of the cobbler, the mule-driver, the cook, the housewife, the soldier or the slave. Language itself is full of metaphors which are really models in that they give 'to airy nothing a local habitation'.

Models have their disadvantages too. No model illustrates the truth at every point, if pressed too far it can falsify truth. Unfortunately people show a tendency to take models too seriously and to invest them with an authority which they cannot possess. The model-maker becomes enamoured of his creature and hangs on to it beyond its useful life. What at first stimulated the imagination eventually deludes it. Every model, analogy, myth or comparison illuminates one aspect of reality at the risk of falsifying another.

Many models have been suggested to describe the essence of traditional teaching. It has been compared to the pouring into a pitcher by means of a funnel some precious liquid. Another figurative comparison is to a sculptor or modeller in clay or to a writer on wax; and frequently, teaching has been compared to gardening and the teacher has been pictured as preparing the soil, watering and feeding the plants, keeping them free from weeds and pruning them where necessary. But the biological model has always been a favourite with teachers who, in Froebel's words, think of their work as 'unfolding, bringing out, lifting into consciousness the divine essence in a child'.[1] Dewey focused attention on problem-solving as the key to education and therefore used the model of a 'forked-road situation'.

[1] Froebel, Friedrich, *The Education of Man*, para. 5.

Benjamin Franklin thought of it as a hollow-log situation with the teacher at one end and the pupil at the other, holding conversation. In all these cases there is some element of truth but when stressed they become absurd.

TEACHING AS INITIATION

In his inaugural address at London University in 1963, Professor R. S. Peters examined some of the models which we have mentioned and went on to suggest that the term 'initiation' would be 'general enough to cover the different types of transaction' which may be identified with education. He disclaimed any intention of producing 'yet another model' which would be 'to sin against the glimmerings of light that may have so far flickered over my treatment of the concept of education'.[2] It is difficult to see why he should be so coy about suggesting a model, even though, as he says, 'education marks out no particular type of transaction between teachers and learners; it states criteria to which such transactions have to conform'.

He gives three such criteria:

1. Education must be initiation into what is worthwhile. Thus Bill Sykes would not count as an educator.
2. It must involve understanding and cognitive perspective. This would rule out rote learning and mechanical training.
3. It must not involve procedures that 'lack wittingness and voluntariness on the part of the learner'.[3] This would rule out conditioning. Indoctrination is a more difficult case but is rejected on the grounds that it 'encourages no criticism or evaluation of beliefs.'[4]

It is clear that the term 'initiation' is intended to draw attention to certain characteristics of education which are found in traditional models. It is a process of 'transmission'. The emphasis of what is transmitted is on knowledge and understanding. The function of the learner is one of 'wittingness and voluntariness'. The 'initiation' emphasises the intention of the teacher and the worth of what he has to offer; and in this sense it is a reaction against child-centred education although it might be taken as an attempt to harmonise the two points of view. It goes some way towards elucidating the key problems of child-centred education: how can the teacher guide

[2] Peters, R. S., 'Education as Initiation', in R. D. Archambault (ed.), *Philosophical Analysis and Education* (Routledge & Kegan Paul, 1966), p. 102.
[3] Peters, R. S., *Ethics and Education* (Allen & Unwin, 1966), p. 45.
[4] *Ibid.*, p. 42.

without directing? how can the pupil discover unless he has some idea of what he is looking for?

Initiation brings to mind certain concrete cases in which it takes place. It is a familiar term with anthropologists in describing the ceremonies and procedures by which, in primitive society, a youth takes his place as an adult member of the tribe or group. Usually there is some test of competence in one or other of the skills deemed necessary for the survival of the tribe. Then there is a ceremony by which the young man indicates that he accepts the authority of the elders, and he must accept without question tribal lore and custom. There is also a religious aspect to primitive man's initiation, in placating hostile spirits and invoking favourable ones. The oath by which he recognises duties and responsibilities has behind it the solemn sanctions of religious belief. Finally there is frequently a test of manhood by which the initiate proves his courage or endurance.

Initiation is also the term normally used when a person joins a Church. Thus in the early Church it was necessary that intending Christians should undergo a period of instruction in doctrine and a trial of moral behaviour. Eventually, on full confession of faith before witnesses, there was a rite signifying their entry into the Church. With the growth of monasticism, initiation came to indicate the process by which a man undertook the vows which made him a member of the brotherhood. The preceding period of training was to give him competence in literary arts, but its chief purpose was to establish 'right' belief essential for salvation.

Initiation into a craft or profession in the Middle Ages still had a strong religious element but the emphasis was more on competence in a skill. Thus the page who attended upon the household of a knight, learnt courtesy to women (at least those of high degree) and obedient service to the knight. He passed from being a page to being a squire, in which role he learnt all the arts deemed appropriate to knighthood, i.e. playing the harp, hunting and fighting. In the case of the more humble craftsman the procedure was basically the same. The apprentice lived in the household of the master-craftsman from whom he learnt the 'mystery' of his craft. He became a journeyman and eventually produced his own masterpiece of work by which he was judged competent to join the guild of master craftsmen.

There are today many relics of traditional initiation in the practices of social groups who wish to emphasise their special status. Hence the ceremonies of ordination, of degree conferment, of entry to clubs and associations, all of which involve some selection of fitness, some period of training, minimum qualifications, moral acceptability or contractual ceremony. The question arises: what relevance has all this to the education of a child in the primary school? Are there any ways in which a primary school can resemble a primitive tribe, a monastic brotherhood, a knightly caste or a craft guild?

Each of these groups believed that they held something corporately which was worth preserving and defending. They were committed to the 'worth-whileness' of their heritage. This gave them an *esprit de corps*, the sense of being an in-group, a camaraderie which bound them together. Their customary rites and procedures were hallowed by long use and given dignity by religious associations. Do the teachers of a primary school feel like that? Should they?

The parallel is easier to make in the case of a university which is defined as 'a community of scholars and research workers who also regard it as their business to initiate others into the pursuit of truth'.[5] Thus the common purpose which holds its members together is that 'they themselves are advancing the frontiers of knowledge' and are 'acknowledged authorities in their field'. To some extent the same might be said about the great public schools and the well-established grammar schools. They have a sense of tradition. They feel they have a heritage to defend. But should primary schools be comparable?

Professor Peters suggests that all forms of education should have the character of initiation and he uses the analogy of a citadel in which the values of civilisation are preserved. Outside the gates are the 'barbarians indifferent to all that constitutes being civilised'. Inside are the teachers trying to get the barbarians inside 'so that they will understand and love what they see when they get there'. Some 'luring' may be necessary 'by using their existing interests', but it is used with the hope that eventually the barbarians will 'develop other interests which were previously never dreamed of'.[6] It is a delusion to think that this is going to be an easy process, because the young initiates have to submit to the rules of the citadel and the educators have 'an uphill task in which there are no short cuts'. The popular insistence that children should be happy 'ignores this brutal fact. People can be happy lying in the sun; but happiness such as this is not the concern of the educator'. 'Being happy' must not be confused with 'living a worthwhile life.'[7]

The concept of initiation seems to be an attempt to bring back into education more rigour, more regard for standards, more regard for the fact that culture is not a soft option but has to be striven for. The question arises: Is it compatible with a system of universal education? How far does it meet the needs of the very young, of the child of below-average intelligence, of the disadvantaged child?

[5] Peters, R. S., *Ethics and Education* (Allen & Unwin, 1966), p. 72.
[6] Peters, R. S., in Archambault *op. cit.*, pp. 107, 109.
[7] *Ibid.*, p. 108.

Professor Peters tries to answer these questions. He agrees that 'a large proportion of the population in Great Britain suffers from an environment which militates against such motivation and cognitive development', and concludes that 'it would be unwise as well as unfair to conclude too soon that education can only be for an élite'.[8] He does concede that the avenues of initiation have to be adapted to the nature of individual children—'hence the relevance of activity methods which cater well for individual idiosyncrasies and divergent rates of growth. Such a "child-centred" approach is as appropriate in dealing with the backward or difficult adolescent as it is at the infant stage. For the crucial difference is not one of age, but of the development of cognitive structure, and of degrees of initiation into public and differentiated modes of thought'.[9] At the same time, he does admit that 'the nature of education can be seriously influenced by its manner of distribution', and this leads him to support those institutions which have taken 'many years to build up and which actually do succeed in initiating children into the forms of thought and awareness, with their built-in standards of excellence, which are constitutive of a quality of life'.[10] So far as primary education is concerned, the argument seems to be that the stage of 'romance' described by A. N. Whitehead should be followed, at the appropriate time, by the stage of 'precision'. Whitehead says that the stage of romance 'is not dominated by systematic procedure' but that the ferment created by immediate 'cognisance of fact' must soon be set in order by the stage of precision.[11] The prospect is a daunting one, no vista of immediate Promised Land, but 'the crunch of standards with all that it entails in blood, sweat and tears'.[12]

Not only is age and intelligence a factor in deciding how a child can be initiated, social class must also be considered. Thus we note:

'The working-class man, who has access only to a limited vocabulary and to a limited set of symbolic structures, literally lives in a different world from the professional man who has a much wider and more varied vocabulary and whose education in the various differentiated forms of thought has continued for nearly a decade longer . . . In learning a language the individual is initiated into a public inheritance which his parents and teachers are inviting him to share'.[13]

[8] *Ibid.*, p. 108.
[9] Peters, R. S., *Ethics and Education*, *op. cit.*, p. 56.
[10] *Ibid.*, p. 137.
[11] Whitehead, A. N., *The Aims of Education* (Free Press Edn, 1967), p. 18.
[12] Peters, R. S., 'Education as Initiation', *op. cit.*, p. 109.
[13] Peters, R. S., *Ethics and Education*, *op. cit.*, pp. 52–3.

It would appear from this that the children of professional people are already over the threshold of the citadel, and that the teacher is already on the inside holding the key to mystery. But to speak of creativity or problem-solving or discovery for the uninitiated is 'cant'.

Clearly it is of some importance to the argument that we should know what is this 'mystery' hidden from the masses. The chief element seems to be contained in the term 'forms of knowledge', which occurs frequently. Over many centuries men have developed a certain number of forms of knowledge, such as history, science and philosophy, which now have an independent and impersonal existence. No one is born with them. No one can obtain them except by being accompanied by one already initiated. Initiation is in any case a relative condition, and the experience of exploring the common world of one or other of these distinctive forms is a shared one. Both teacher and learner have to submit to the canons or standards which have been evolved and which have to be publicly recognised by all who claim to possess the mystery. Inherent in the concept of initiation is that it should be arduous and take many years—indeed, that it requires some of the old Puritan virtues of enterprise, orderliness, thoroughness and perseverance, for which 'there is much to be said—especially in education'.[14] Inherent also is the concern of the initiators for what they have; they must themselves be committed to the standards to which they introduce others. In truth, their conviction that their standards are of value outweighs any consideration for the immediate wants of the initiates. For instance, we read:

'A teacher, like a guardian in relation to a ward, who is mindful of children's interests, is not necessarily exercised about what they actually want or are interested in, or their hobbies; he (or she) is concerned about protecting them in what he thinks they have a right to pursue or with ensuring that they pursue what is both worthwhile and suitable for them, i.e. beneficial for them. He therefore has to consider not only what is in general worthwhile but also what the potentialities and capacities are of the particular children for whom he is responsible.'[15]

Finally something must be said about the ceremonial or ritualistic side of initiation. Professor Peters treats this as incidental but nevertheless important. Thus he says:

'Lessons are obviously not quite the same as initiation ceremonies; but they are certainly most effective when they share some of their

[14] Peters, R. S., 'Education as Initiation', *op. cit.*, p. 110.
[15] Peters, R. S., *Ethics and Education*, *op. cit.*, p. 168.

atmosphere . . . They are at best extrinsic aids which facilitate the task of the teacher. They intimate, at second hand, as it were, that something of interest and of value is at stake; they may provide an atmosphere which may permit a teacher to get his pupils to enjoy first-hand experience of what is to be marked out.'[16] Thus

ritual has something of the same function for children as it had for pages or apprentices:

'children have to be initiated into forms of thought and behaviour, the rationale of which they cannot at first understand . . . Rituals are a method by which the importance of a practice can be marked out and children made to feel that it is something in which they should participate. It is surely better than bribing or goading them.'[17]

INITIATION IN PRIMARY EDUCATION

Many points in the initiation model of teaching may be applied in university education; rather less in secondary schools and only to a limited extent in primary schools. However, there are certain aspects which call for comment. The idea of a school as a fraternity of people holding roughly the same ideals and sharing in a common venture is very attractive, and is in line with the modern trend away from the isolated class teacher system. To find an example we may, unfortunately, have to go outside the state system to the Rudolf Steiner schools. There are at present eighteen English-speaking Steiner schools and fifty others in different parts of the world. The full course consists of kindergarten (4–6$\frac{1}{2}$ years), middle school (6$\frac{1}{2}$–14$\frac{1}{2}$ years) and upper school (14$\frac{1}{2}$–18$\frac{1}{2}$ years). These schools are based on the philosophy of Rudolf Steiner which emphasises the spiritual nature of man and of the world, and devotional activities are practised each day. There is no head teacher but the school is administered by the teaching staff as a body, called the College of Teachers. They arrange the curriculum and meet regularly to share experiences and no member is in a position of authority over another. Each day begins with what is called a 'main lesson' of two hours; a particular subject is taught in this way for several weeks, at the end of which another subject is chosen. The rest of the day is taken up with practice lessons and recreative activities such as eurythmy, music and arts and crafts. The teacher aims very deliberately at creating an atmosphere of emotional security so that no child can feel he is failing or falling behind others. The class teacher is responsible for one group of children throughout the whole of their time

[16] *Ibid.*, p. 260.
[17] *Ibid.*, p. 318.

in the kindergarten or middle schools and therefore has every chance of making a close personal contact with each child. What holds the school together is its sense of shared ideals.

It is certainly true that junior children can be introduced quite early to the basic 'forms of knowledge', if we take this to mean the disciplines which have, in fact, been developed systematically over the centuries and, in particular, the grounds which each of them has for the validity of its statements. The problem would be to know how or in what order they should be introduced to young children. Most teachers would feel that prior to any attempt to introduce these forms of knowledge the child needs to be able to read with facility and understanding. This must be the key by which the child opens the door to mathematics, science and history and it is relevant even to the arts. We might well say that the teacher is trying to lure the child into the citadel where books are readily available. Some children, the bright ones and the ones already initiated, will not need much luring and most children sense the importance of being able to read and are therefore well-motivated. The task of the teacher is to make the initiation process as pleasant and easy as possible. Much work has been done to find the easiest way—phonics, look and say, ITA, and linguistics—but increasingly it is realised that the teacher is more important than the method. What will suit one child will confuse another. What is helpful at the beginning may be an obstacle later on. Reading cannot be mastered by 'blood, sweat and tears' nor by mechanical drill, but by seeing it as fun. The inherent weakness of many scientifically conceived reading schemes is that they are boring or irrelevant to most children. The signal of success is not when a child can read a passage aloud, but when he begins to read silently and for pleasure. When so much emphasis is put on reading aloud both teacher and child overlook the fact that reading is a process of thinking. Initiation means introducing the hesitant learner to books within his capacity and appealing to his imagination, and the attraction must be in the words and not in the accompanying pictures. There are few teachers in the primary school who do not have some children with reading difficulties or children who are technically able to read but reluctant to do so.

The crux of the argument about initiation is whether the initiative should come from the teacher or from the child. Professor Peters thinks it must come from the teacher, who alone is possessed of the worthwhile knowledge and must decide how to approach it. Unfortunately, history gives us little warrant for thinking that teachers always know what is best for the child. For centuries children have been forcibly initiated into the cultural inheritance, but all have not benefited. Whatever truth there may be in the existence of logically ordered systems of knowledge, we cannot put old heads on young shoulders. The logical approach to learning may be suitable for the expert but for the beginner we may need to take a more psychological and indirect approach. The longest way round may be the shortest way home in the end. That is why the emphasis in modern primary education has changed to discovery which, as the *Plowden Report* says, is 'a useful shorthand description of many of the ideas involved'.[18]

The project method is a good illustration of the difference of approach. Although, frequently, projects as used in schools are strongly teacher-directed the essence of this method is that it should arise from a felt need of the children, and be completely open-ended so that the teacher has to feel his way with the class and individual children within it may work out their own salvation. The assumption upon which it is based is the 'natural' curiosity of the child. Rousseau made great play of this: Emile should learn geography from his own environment and Rousseau claims 'no doubt he will require some guidance but very little, and that without his knowing it . . . what he needs is not an exact knowledge of local topography but how to find out for himself' (*Emile*, Book III). To say that a project should be child-conceived and child-developed does not imply that it may not be sparked off by something the teacher does or says. For instance, it is unlikely that a class of juniors will hit upon a subject like Red Indians or Vikings by themselves, but stories or pictures of one or the other might well provide the initial stimulus and have the great advantage of giving full scope to the kind of fantasies young children love.

The initiation which is required for a system of universal education must be more broadly based than the traditional forms of knowledge and it must be into worthwhile activities—and to be worthwhile they must necessarily have a cognitive perspective. The activity which every child will be engaged in during his life is the activity of sex. Whether it is worthwhile activity or not will depend upon the way he is initiated into it. Relation between the sexes is so funda-mental to human conduct that it would be strange if it did not have some place in the initiation process. Various arguments might be raised against giving it a place in primary education. The familiar one is that sex education is best left to the parents, and that even if they fail in their obligations children cannot help but pick up from mass media and elsewhere all the knowledge they require. Another argument is that sex education is best left to the secondary stage when the onset of puberty makes it relevant. Yet another point is that sex education either goes too far or falls short of what is neces-sary. The disputes over Martin Cole's film are directed against what

[18] *Plowden Report*, 1967, para. 549.

is regarded as unhealthy frankness, approaching the pornographic. On the other hand, the treatment of sex education which ignores the human and emotional factors is quite inadequate; indeed there are arguments against treating it as a separate subject in its own right because of the artificiality of such a treatment. The truth is that any teacher should feel able to initiate his pupils into some aspect or another of sex—in biology or health education the make-up of the natural world, including the human, will come in; physical education will cover many aspects of physiology; moral education (under whatever heading it may come) will be concerned with inter-personal responsibility; in art there should be the aesthetic appreciation of the human form, male and female; in geography and social studies such questions as population control and family structure come in; and literature provides abundant opportunity for dealing with the emotional side of sex activity. It is obvious that, provided the will is present, every teacher could take sex as part of his initiating responsibility. As to the point about its inappropriateness in the primary school, it should be noted that many girls will reach puberty at the age of 11 and that the middle school will extend the age range and make some preliminary teaching, especially in biology, very desirable. For teachers who fear to venture on to controversial ground because of parental opposition there are now broadcasting programmes for which parent approval can be specifically sought.

It is important that sex education should not be narrowly confined to the physiology of sex. The whole question of the relationship between men and women is one of the most important in life. Boys and girls need to realise as soon as possible the complementary nature of their relationship with each other. The moral question, too, is crucial, since in sex, as in any other relationship, other people's needs are as important as one's own, and this should be the deciding factor in discussing possible patterns. The teacher should consciously seek to foster sensitivity towards those aspects of sexual relationships where moral judgements may be required. Thus, the aim of sex education is not to dispense information about this or that, but to help children at all stages of their life to satisfy their sexual needs in the fullest possible sense. Certainly, it should not stop at anatomy.

FURTHER READING

BBC, *School Broadcasting and Sex Education in the Primary School* (BBC, 1971).
Clark, Berna (ed.,) *Books for Primary Children: Annotated List* (School Library Association, 1969).
Culling, George, *Projects for the Middle School* (Lutterworth, 1972).

Dearden, R. F., *Philosophy of Primary Education* (Routledge & Kegan Paul, 1968).

Fellows, M. S., *Projects for Schools* (Museum Press, 1965).

Hare, Richard, *Know How: A Student's Guide to Project Work* (Intertext Books, 1970).

Haslam, Kenneth, *Learning in the Primary School* (Allen & Unwin, 1971).

Hirst, P. H., 'Liberal Education and the Nature of Knowledge', in R. D. Archambault, *Philosophical Analysis and Education* (Routledge & Kegan Paul, 1965).

Hoare, R. J., *Topic Work with Books* (Chapman, 1971).

Horner, P. H., *Reading* (Heinemann, 1972).

Kent, Graeme, *Projects in the Primary School* (Batsford, 1968).

King, A. R. and Brownell, J. A., *The Curriculum and the Disciplines of Knowledge* (John Wiley, 1966).

Macmillan, C. J. B., and Nelson, T. W. (eds), *Concepts of Teaching* (Rand McNally, 1968).

Melnik, Amelia and Merritt, John, *Reading Today and Tomorrow* (ULP, 1972).

Moyle, D., and L., *Modern Innovations in the Teaching of Reading* (ULP, 1971).

Peters, R. S., 'Mental Health as an Educational Aim', in Hollins, T. H. B., (ed.), *Aims in Education* (Manchester Univ. Press, 1964).

Perry, Leslie R., 'What is an Educational Situation', in Archambault, R.D. *Philosophical Analysis and Education* (Routledge & Kegan Paul, 1966).

Ramsey, E. T., *Models and Mystery* (OUP, 1964).

Richmond, W. K., *The Teaching Revolution* (Methuen, 1967).

Scheffler, Israel, 'Philosophical Models of Teaching', in Peters, R. S. (ed.), *The Concept of Education* (Routledge & Kegan Paul, 1967).

Scheffler, Israel, *The Language of Education* (Blackwell, 1960).

Smith, B. Othanel, 'A Concept of Teaching', in Smith, B. O., and Ennis, R. H., *Language and Concepts in Education* (Rand McNally, 1967).

Southgate V. and Roberts, G. R., *Reading: Which Approach?* (ULP, 1970).

Steiner, Rudolf, *A Modern Art of Education* (Rudolf Steiner Press, Revised Edn, 1972).

Tansley, A. E., *Reading and Remedial Reading* (Routledge & Kegan Paul, 1967).

Wilson, John, *Logic and Sexual Morality* (Penguin, 1965).

Worrall, P. *et. al.*, *Teaching from Strength* (Hamish Hamilton, 1970).

Chapter 4

Evaluation

EVALUATION OF PROGRESSIVE EDUCATION

The evaluation of results is important in every organisation as a means of judging whether objectives have been achieved. No factory could continue in business without some way of measuring profits or production. No corporate body could flourish without some periodic assessment of numerical or financial stability. The school system is no exception, even though its numbers are compulsorily maintained and its results cannot be quantitatively measured. One could argue that the fundamental justification for any corporate body is the happiness and virtue of those involved in it but that this is peculiarly true of an educational establishment. Nevertheless, schools cannot opt out of the necessity for demonstrating that they achieve what they set out to do. In 1962 a report was issued (the *Morris Report*) entitled *Investment for National Survival* which gave as the objectives of national education that 'individuals should become better citizens' so that 'our national economy should not increasingly fall behind those of our rivals'. The first is very difficult to demonstrate and it is impossible to show a direct relationship between education and economic growth. None the less, education is an investment of money, persons and material resources from which it is reasonable to expect dividends to accrue, but the constant demand for increasing investment does imply an obligation to demonstrate dividends.

A hundred years ago Robert Lowe made his famous statement about the elementary school system, 'If it cannot be cheap at least let us make it efficient'. The revised code which set out to do this demonstrated clearly the ill-effects of taking a narrow set of criteria for efficiency. The attempt to standardise achievement in the 'three Rs' and to pay teachers accordingly dehumanised both them and their pupils, but the abolition of payment by results did not solve the problem of finding more valid criteria by which the 'customers' of education might be satisfied.

Though it may be impossible to demonstrate educational success in terms of better citizens or national economic expansion, there is one aspect of its functions that would seem to be amenable to assessment, i.e. the function of sorting people out according to their abilities and aptitudes. It could be claimed that schools fulfil a necessary sorting-out function by providing a 'ladder of opportunity' for bright youngsters from any class or rank. They ensure that square pegs do not fill round holes and that a natural meritocracy is created which fulfils social justice. Hence the phenomenal growth of the public examination system. If the success of the system were to be judged by the number of children passing public examination at various levels it would be impressive, yet many arguments could be raised against this yardstick. The fallibility of tests and examinations, whether of innate intelligence or of scholastic performance, is acknowledged. It is clear that success in them is closely related to social background and does not prove superior ability. The modern movement is towards deferring selection by merit as long as possible and giving multiple chances to the slow developer and the socially disadvantaged. The ladder of opportunity may give joy to the fortunate few but pain and resentment to the rejected many. The emphasis on sorting out may well be the main cause for the failure of education to capture the imagination of the majority of children. These are some of the arguments which have led to the comprehensive system of secondary education, to the reaction against streaming in primary schools and to the abandoning in most areas of 11-plus selection.

The theory of equal opportunity must be reinterpreted to mean that every child shall be given an equal opportunity to develop in his own way and to the maximum. But this implies that individual differences can be measured and individual potentialities diagnosed. Educational diagnosis might then be thought of as parallel with medical diagnosis where all the relevant factors are brought together —age, sex, domestic background, medical history, blood pressure, heart-beat, height, weight and so on. Effective treatment of symptoms depends upon efficient assessment of conditions. It could be argued that the same applies in educational terms to children, teachers, classes, schools and systems. Each is more or less healthy from an educational point of view and each can be diagnosed.

To specify treatment is not so easy. Whereas medical treatment can be put to the test of a return of health or mobility, and drugs can be tested before use, educational procedures are far less amenable to confirmation. This is one of the reasons for the fact that far less is spent on educational than on medical research. The results of failure in medical research, as in the case of thalidomide, are obvious and dramatic but it is very difficult—control groups notwithstanding

—to show that one method of education is superior to another. It all depends on personal relationships. To take another case, an industrialist may make an inquiry into profitability by examining such things as output, use of plant, labour, marketing and so on, and with the aid of cost accountants, motion experts, and market consultants come to a reasonable conclusion about remedial measures. The amount of money involved in education may be much larger but the objectives are not clear-cut, nor are the criteria for success obvious or the results measurable in time. Consequently there are many alibis for failure, many excuses for inertia and results are unpredictable.

Take, for instance, the *Plowden Report* which has not only been hailed on all sides as a most constructive document but whose recommendations are backed up by a second volume of statistical evidence. If we look at the main conclusions we see how tentative they are.

1. The Report concentrates on the education of young children, and of the youngest children in particular. The interest in this subject is demonstrated by the government proposals for a massive expansion of nursery education, by the increasing attention given to pre-school playgroups and by the proposals for parity of conditions in primary and secondary schools.

2. The *Report* endorses the revolution in primary education. This has stimulated widespread interest among teachers and the general public as to the character of the revolution, as is illustrated by the setting up of teachers' centres, and by experiments in buildings and equipment.

3. The *Report* speaks strongly in favour of increased co-operation between home and school. This has stimulated activity in many directions. Books and pamphlets on the subject have proliferated; organisations such as the Confederation for the Advancement of State Education, the Cambridge Advisory Centre for Education and the National Federation of Parent Teacher Associations have been stimulated; and a Home and School Council has been formed to press forward the reforms recommended by the *Report*.

4. The *Report* recommends that there should be positive discrimination in favour of the educational priority areas and that more help should be given over the whole field of housing, health and social services as well as in education. This has resulted in increased government expenditure on schools in these areas and in proposals for urban renewal and community development. Indeed, there are tentative efforts to bring into being a new type of community school, engaging the co-operation of parents directly. Various research

projects have been started to investigate ways of helping children to overcome their handicaps.[1]

5. The *Report* recommends a re-organisation of primary education into 'first school' and 'middle school' and there is a growing movement to implement this.

6. A great many recommendations are put forward concerning the training, qualifications and distribution of primary teachers, and this has been followed up by the *James Report* and by government proposals for the re-organisation of training and for in-service training.

However much we may agree with these conclusions it has to be admitted that it is extremely difficult to evaluate them especially when they are applied to the primary school. Here education is now relatively free from the tyrannies of the past, from 'three R' standards, 11-plus selection, and rigid timetables and syllabuses. There is much less insistence than formerly on spelling, handwriting, tables and neatness generally, and in their place enthusiasm for creative writing, practical maths and free art. These things are very much in line with the *Plowden* approach, but from time to time there are complaints from parents and the general public of a falling-off in standards which cannot be shrugged off as mere reaction. Without evaluation, informal methods will be brought into disrepute and in the course of time new fetters will be forged to eliminate slipshodness.

THE SCOPE AND LIMITATIONS OF PRESENT METHODS OF ASSESSMENT

As a generalisation it may be said that modern primary teachers are not so meticulous about marking as were their predecessors. It is said that too many red marks on a child's writing are discouraging, that spelling must be corrected selectively and that emphasis on grammar and handwriting stifles creative expression. A personal knowledge of individuals is said to be preferable to lists of marks out of ten. This may be so, but the size of classes makes it easy for individuals to be overlooked unless adequate records are kept of individual progress. To be adequate the records should be satisfactory for the various purposes to which they may be put, such as:

1. Helping the teacher to see what is happening.
2. Giving the next teacher or the head teacher enough data to sum up the state of affairs.

[1] e.g., a research programme under Dr Halsey, Nuffield College, Oxford, to investigate areas of need in Birmingham, Dundee, Liverpool, London, Sutherland and the West Riding and the 'Compensatory Education Project' at Swansea under Professor Gittins.

3. As material to be passed on to parents as a basis for co-operation.

For each of these purposes different kinds of assessment may be necessary in order to communicate the most significant information. This raises the most important value of assessment: its feed-back. This occurs at every level, from the individual child becoming aware of his progress, to the Chief Education Officer determining policy. Above all, feed-back is important for the teacher because it enables him at every stage of his programme to evaluate his success and to modify his plans accordingly. No programme should be carried through without constant evaluation and consequent modification.

Of all the conclusions provided by research into learning theory none is more sure than the importance of the learner's awareness of success or failure. This is generally held to be a more powerful reinforcement than extrinsic rewards or punishments. The point is that evaluation by the teacher should lead to self-evaluation by the learner. This implies that assessment must be made as soon as possible after the work has been completed, that it must be made in a form which the learner can readily understand and that on the whole it should be encouraging rather than discouraging.

This raises the problem of how far we should praise inferior work. Genuine learning depends on honesty and even little children can soon detect the hypocrisy of unmerited praise. The question here is: What do we mean by 'merited'? Does not a naturally dull child deserve more commendation for doing his best than a bright one who could do better? Good and bad are, after all, relative terms. None the less, no child is hurt by being made aware that there are objective standards appropriate to excellence in his particular group. Thus, there must come into all evaluation of children's work a subjective element of approval and an objective element of judgement. Some teachers try to combine the two by giving two marks— one for effort and another for performance. This is apt to be clumsy. Others avoid numerical or literal marks altogether and confine themselves to comments. Comments look as if they are entirely subjective: 'Well tried and quite interesting', for instance; but they soon become standardised and just as mechanical as marks, and they take much longer to write.

In trying to strike a balance between objectivity and subjectivity or between performance and effort it is suggested that the teacher should give priority to teaching feed-back rather than to accurate judgement. Thus, if a low mark or grade or comment has to be given on objective grounds, it should normally be softened by a favourable comment on whatever is 'lovely and of good report' which, although sometimes not easy to find, is worth the effort. Children who do badly have become inured to disapproval. They need encouragement more desperately than those who do well. The temptation is to let comments of approval become stereotyped and not personalised.

Wherever possible pupils should be encouraged to make their own evaluation. This not only saves time, but is generally more effective than the teacher's correction because it involves conscious effort on the part of the pupil to look back. Teacher's marks frequently fail to do this. If mistakes can be rectified at once they do not become habits; it is feasible to provide children with a marking code for calculations and one-word answer assignments, and to encourage each child to keep his own cumulative record of progress. One of the great arguments in favour of programmed learning is that at every step the child is aware of success or failure and can check his own learning. Especially valuable from this point of view are the branching programmes, which take the learner back if he is failing to understand a step in the argument and do not leave him with the feeling that getting the right answer is a matter of luck in choosing the right alternative. What is claimed on behalf of programmed learning is that it lessens hopeless floundering. It makes learning seem easy

In giving assignments the teacher wants to aim for trial and success not trial and error. He should try to envisage the kind of response likely to come from the below-average child and then perhaps change its form so that the right answer is, if not certain, likely.

However, getting the right answer is not the only thing that needs marking and much of the written work done by children is of a descriptive nature. The custom of writing things out 'in rough' first and then making a 'fair copy' seems to have died out but there is some justification for it if it leads children to be critical of their own work. The chief weakness of present methods of assessment is their failure to bring about self-evaluation, and this particularly concerns the half-finished piece of work on single sheets of paper. Sometimes the sheets are fastened together in a folder, but, whether they are in this form or in an exercise book, what is lacking is any sense of continuity. The child is not encouraged to edit his work, to develop it from one stage to another, to incorporate several discrete pieces into a theme, or to develop ideas over a period of time.

OBJECTIVE AND SUBJECTIVE ASSESSMENT

All assessment has objective and subjective elements. Assessment is objective in so far as it depends upon criteria independent of individual judgement, i.e. if it has publicly accepted standards. For instance, correct spelling does not depend upon individual choice but upon the authority of the dictionary; correct grammar is not a matter of preference but of normal convention; and factual correctness can be verified by reference to an authority such as an atlas. In mathematics the appeal is to logical necessity; in science it is to empirical evidence such as that provided by a thermometer. Here there can be no question of marking something right which is patently wrong simply to encourage. Even an approximation to a right answer must be marked in accordance with what it is reasonable to accept, as in measuring. For every objective judgement there is a court of appeal to which both teacher and pupil must submit, and the judgement, to be fair, must be free from kindness or partiality just as much as from caprice or prejudice. That truth and falsehood are stark alternatives is a lesson every child must learn. In objective testing there can always be an authoritative reference.

However, objectivity is limited. In spelling, for instance, there may be alternative forms; grammatical conventions are always changing; a child's dictionary is often misleading; textbooks are frequently out of date or simply wrong. The logical necessity of mathematics and the empirical evidence of science may seem to be irrefutable but mistakes can be made in both fields. However, the problem is that most significant questions do not admit of right/wrong answers. Think, for instance, of the trouble the American Supreme Court has in deciding what the American Constitution means. At the lower level of questions in school there are many that are open-ended or that require explanation rather than accuracy. There are areas of judgement in which even relative objectivity is subject to emotional bias. There are moral and aesthetic questions where reasons are looked for. Any question involving better or worse, more or less, or reasons for and against, demands a measure of interpretation. In all such cases a subjective element comes in.

All questions have to be selected. This means that the questioner thinks they are worth while or appropriate. He must have some purpose in mind and this gives a subjective element. This mixture of objective and subjective elements may be illustrated by reference to an individual intelligence test. The Terman and Merrill Revised Stanford-Binet Intelligence Test gives the following question for Year VII:

2. Similarities; Two Things
Procedure: Say, 'in what way are . . . and . . . alike?'
   (*a*) Wood and coal
   (*b*) Apple and orange

  (*c*) Ship and motor-car
  (*d*) Iron and silver

Then comes the following instruction. 'It is permissible to repeat the original question or to add, "How are they the same?" or "In what way are they alike?" When a difference is given for (*a*) say, "No, I want you to tell me how they are alike".'

In the scoring manual the following directions are given: 'In scoring the similarities test, any real likeness, whether fundamental or superficial, is counted satisfactory. Samples of plus and minus follow:

  (*a*) Wood and coal
  Plus. "Both burn." "Both keep you warm." "They burn and are both wood." "You could put both of them in the fire." "Burn coal with wood." "Both come from the ground." "Both hard." "Both got the letter 'o'.", etc.
  Minus. "Both black." "Both the same colour." "Coal's dirty and wood is dirty." "You can't break them." "Coal burns better."'

Since, as the authors of the test say, 'All forms of the comparison test have shown high correlation with total score' one might expect that it would be highly objective, but the subjective element in deciding how 'fundamental or superficial' a likeness is must bring in subjective judgements.[2]

 A few years ago problem questions in mathematics were very popular but how often was the child bewildered by the wording which, if not ambiguous, was difficult to understand! How often in more recent years have questions on work-card assignments lacked clarity or appropriateness! How often are questions of 'the Why' type difficult to mark because of the wide range of possible answers! The subjective element comes into the choice and wording of questions just as much as into the marking of the answers. At each stage problems of objectivity and subjectivity arise and have to be considered.

1. *Selecting the questions* Is the question suitable for particular children, worthwhile in itself, clearly expressed, and likely to lead to profitable feed-back?

2. *Marking the answers* What is the source of authority for correctness? What degree of accuracy can be expected? Does the answer

[2] Terman L. M. and Merrill, M. A. *Measuring Intelligence* (Harrap, 1955), pp. 98 and 228.

reveal understanding? What kind and length of marking scale is being used? If comments are used, what is their purpose? In what way is feed-back possible?

3. *Keeping Records* Do they reveal progress or lack of it over a period of time? To whom are they revealed and for what purpose, i.e. are they used for diagnostic or motivational purposes?

The fundamental factor in all evaluating processes is their effect upon the learner. Marking is not an end in itself. It must be used as feed-back both for teacher and pupil.

Statistical Tools of Evaluation
Teachers often hesitate to use statistical methods because they lack mathematical ability. In fact, a high level of such ability is not so important as an understanding of the chief concepts. Thus a 'frequency distribution' simply means an analysis of the way in which marks are distributed. For instance, a group of thirty children might be marked on a five-point scale as follows:

Number of children	Mark given	Percentage of Whole
3	A	10
8	B	27
15	C	50
3	D	10
1	E	3
Total 30		100

This could be illustrated in graphical form, as shown in Figure 3.

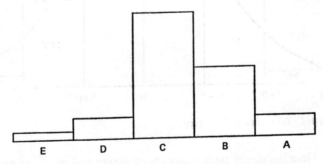

Figure 3   Frequency distribution – a five-point scale for marking children

It would indicate that the distribution was 'skewed' towards the upper range but not markedly so, and that, in fact, the whole range was being used. The question that arises is whether these marks, or indeed any others, are valid, i.e. do they indicate truthfully any objective standards? The answer is that all standards are relative. They may be relative to what the teacher thinks his class is capable of, or what an individual child is capable of, or to what he thinks an average child of this age is capable of. However, there are two kinds of objective standards which may be used as a rough yardstick for small groups.

The first is known as the curve of normal frequency This is a mathematical curve which has a bell shape, i.e. rising high in the middle and tapering off symmetrically on each side. Empirically it is found that the distribution of a great many human characteristics conforms more or less closely to this abstract curve. Therefore it gives a tentative guide in marking a small group. The larger the group the more correspondence there would be and therefore with a small group it can only be approximate. If we divide the curve of normal frequency into six segments the percentages are symmetrical, as shown by the following diagram:

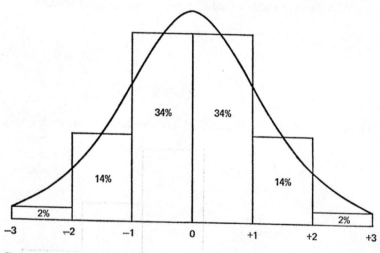

Figure 4 Curve of normal frequency

Here the centre point marks the average and there are deviations on either side which are called standard deviations. Thus, between 0 and +1 standard deviations, approximately 34 per cent of scores will occur; between +1 and +2, 14 per cent; and between +2 and +3, 2 per cent. Similarly this occurs with deviations below the zero line. So on the five-point scale something like 68 per cent would be marked C; 14 per cent B; and 2 per cent A; 14 per cent D and 2 per cent E. In the class of thirty children, therefore, we might expect the following theoretical distribution: A—1, B—4, C—20, D—4, E—1. Statistically about two-thirds of any sample should be clustered around the average mark. Of course, in practice other factors will operate and it would be unusual to find an actual distribution like this.

The second kind of objective standard which might be taken as a guide to the marking of a particular sample is the standardised test. A test is standardised if it is given to a sufficiently large number of testees and if the sample is a representative one. A test is said to be *reliable* if similar results would be given if it should be repeated in similar conditions and *valid* if its results correlate fairly closely with the results of other comparable tests. The scores of standardised tests can be expressed in two ways, either using 100 to indicate the average or zero line and a figure of approximately 15 to represent one standard deviation, or in terms of years. Thus, a child taking a standardised intelligence test with a score of 80 would be slightly below low average while a child with a chronological age of 8 and a reading age of 7 would be about one year behind the average child in his age group.

A standardised test score will help a teacher to compare his own standard of marking with a relatively objective standard. Certainly it will alert him to any pronounced backwardness in a particular child in comparison with his contemporaries. Whether the child is under-achieving in relation to his intelligence quotient is more difficult to assess, but in general there should be some correspondence between intelligence level and achievement level. Some standardised tests are comparatively simple to administer, for example, the Schonell Word Recognition Test, but not so revealing of reading ability as a test such as the Neale Reading Test which takes a number of factors into account. Similarly, a test of intelligence which includes both verbal and non-verbal material, such as the Wechsler Intelligence Test for Children (WISC), probably gives a more accurate measure than one which includes only one or the other. There are standardised tests available for every aspect of the basic subjects, i.e. reading and mathematics; and in addition there is one for concept formation (the Boehm Basic Concept Test) and a number for various aspects of emotional development.

Standardised tests are a useful check on the more subjective marking of the teacher. On the other hand there is a danger of too much objectivity and permanence being ascribed to them. For instance, it is now known that IQ scores can be considerably altered by suitable training and that they do not represent something innate and fixed by nature.

INDIVIDUAL DIAGNOSIS

Amongst teachers there is difference of opinion about the necessity for keeping detailed records of individual children. Some argue that personal relationships between teacher and pupil are best kept at the intuitive, not the clinical, level. Whatever truth there may be in this, the fact is that teachers frequently have 'problem' children to deal with and have inadequate data for doing so adequately, and that there are not enough child guidance resources available. Consequently, these children tend to pass from one teacher to another as they go up the school, getting gradually more and more maladjusted, when a little help at the right time might have saved the situation. Apart from the troublesome pupils there are those who opt out of the race, so to speak, the withdrawn ones. The Report of Joyce Morris (1959) estimated that some 45 per cent of 7-year-old children were not fluent readers who tend to become worse, not better, as they grow older and who finish up by rejecting the values that school stands for. They are the young delinquents of the future. But failure in reading or in any other aspect of school work is easily taken for granted as being inevitable.

If, for such children, there is a case for keeping records which will serve as diagnostic tools, then there is an argument for standardising the form of those records. This is not only a help to the teacher but also a basis for a cumulative record throughout a child's school career by which the total school staff can be involved in a guidance programme. Such records can be passed on from teacher to teacher so that the details are gradually built up over the years. The ideal of a child-centred education must depend upon careful diagnosis of individual children's problems.

Each child has behind him three backgrounds which interact together. First there is his personal background: age, medical history, address, interests, hobbies and experiences. Second there is his family background: position in family, parents and home conditions. Third there is his school background: attendance, change of schools, standardised test scores, class tests expressed in standardised form and literal grading in aesthetic and social skills.

From time to time teachers will make comments on a child's attitude to school work and concerning difficult periods in his life. These comments will be the result of attempts to counsel him.

The counselling function of teachers is a difficult one. The relationship between teacher and pupil cannot be of the intimate kind which we associate with the home. As the *Plowden Report* says, 'a teacher cannot and should not give the deep personal love that each child needs from his parents' (paragraph 137). R. S. Peters also argues for a formal relationship between teacher and pupils since, as he says, 'in a teaching situation love must be of a type that is appropriate to the special type of relationship in which the teacher is placed, to his concept of them as pupils rather than as sons or brothers'.[3] But what of the child who feels rejected by his parents or who feels unwanted by anyone, at least temporarily? If love is too strong a word, approval might be taken as the key to the counselling role of a teacher. Thus, A. S. Neill says, 'A good teacher does not draw out; he gives out, and what he gives out is love. And by love I mean approval, or, if you like, friendliness, good nature. The good teacher not only understands the child: he approves of him'.[4]

SOCIOMETRIC EVALUATION — *abilities*

Nevertheless, the teacher with thirty or more children to care for is limited in the amount of time he can spend with individuals. Much of his time and energy must be devoted to studying the dynamics of the group. The children's relationships with each other are probably as therapeutic as any counselling the teacher can do and part of his evaluation work is to discover how affinities can be fostered and antipathies lessened. A familiar tool in this respect is the sociometric test in which each child is asked to write down the name of the child whom he would most like to work with or to sit next to, or accompany on an outing. From these preferences a map of personal relationships can be drawn up showing which children are mutually attracted, which children are the 'stars' drawing to themselves the regard of several others, and which are the isolated ones who are chosen by no one. This information will enable the teacher to select groups with a natural leader, to put mutual friends together and to find opportunities for isolated children to become involved in co-operative activities. Sociometric grouping has to be considered in relation to ability grouping. For some purposes it is an advantage to have a homogeneous group working together, but, on the other hand, there is much evidence showing the ill-effects of streaming on those who are placed in the lowest group whether they are called the remedial group, the non-readers or simply 'backward'.

[3] Peters, R. S., 'Education as Initiation', in Archambault, R. D., *Philosophical Analysis and Education* (Routledge & Kegan Paul), p. 105.
[4] Neill, A. S., *The Problem Teacher* (Herbert Jenkins, 1939), p. 11.

FURTHER READING

Abercrombie, M. L. J., *Aims and Techniques of Group Teaching* (Society for Research into Higher Education, 1971).

Bloom, B. S., *Taxonomy of Educational Objectives* (*Cognitive*) (D. McKay, 1956).

Bloom, B. S., *Taxonomy of Educational Objectives* (*Affective*) (D. McKay, 1964).

Brown, F. G., *Measurement and Evaluation* (Peacock, Illinois, 1971).

Dean, Joan, *Recording Children's Progress* (Macmillan, 1972).

Eggleston, J. F., and Kerr, J. F., *Studies in Assessment* (English Univ. Press, 1969).

Foster, John, *Recording Individual Progress* (Macmillan, 1971).

Griffiths, S. R. and Downes, L. W., *Educational Statistics for Beginners* (Methuen, 1969).

Holt, John, *How Children Fail* (Pitman, 1964).

Hughes, Patrick M., *Guidance and Counselling* (Pergamon, 1971).

Lunn, Joan, *Streaming in the Primary School* (NFER, 1970).

Macintosh, H. G., and Morrison, K. B., *Objective Testing* (ULP, 1969).

McIntosh, D. M., *Statistics for Teachers* (Pergamon, 1963).

Morris, Joyce, *Standards and Progress in Reading* (NFER, 1966).

Noar, Gertrude, *Individualised Instruction: Every Child a Winner* (John Wiley, 1972).

Peters, R. S. (ed.), *Perspectives on Plowden* (Routledge & Kegan Paul, 1969).

Pidgeon, D. A., *Evaluation of Achievement* (Macmillan, 1972).

Preston, P., *Plowden for Parents* (ACE, 57 Gt Russell St., Cambridge 1969).

Schofield, Harry, *Assessment and Testing* (Allen & Unwin, 1972).

Stones, E. (ed), *Readings in Educational Psychology* (Methuen, 1970).

Thelen, A. H., *Classroom Teaching for Teachability, Inter-class Groups* (John Wiley, 1967).

Tyler, Leona E., *Tests and Measurements* (Prentice Hall, 1963).

Wilhelms, Fred T., 'Evaluation as Feedback', in Hooper, Richard, *The Curriculum* (Oliver & Boyd, 1971).

Chapter 5

Experience

The close connection between education and experience has always been recognised but it has usually been interpreted as meaning sense experience. There is the dictum attributed to Aristotle, 'There is nothing in the mind which was not first in the senses.' Francis Bacon claimed that sense experience of nature was the only 'true key' to science. In a picturesque phrase he says that experience of nature will provide 'the highest link of the chain which must needs be tied to the foot of Jupiter's chair'.[1] Comenius made sense experience the foundation of his *Great Didactic*, saying, 'Those things that are placed before the intelligence of the young, must be "real" things and not the shadows of things . . . and by the term I mean determinate and useful things that can make an impression on the senses and on the imagination.'[2] Then we have John Locke's famous comparison of the human mind as being at birth a blank tablet (*tabula rasa*) on to which ideas are imprinted by sensations and reflection on them.[3] Rousseau is always scathing about an education depending on words and books rather than on the evidence of the senses. He makes his ideal parent say that it is not from books that her young son will gain ideas, but from the impressions of his senses.[4]

However none of these writers really explained how it comes about that sensations can be transformed into ideas. Locke, for instance, speaks of sensations and reflection on them but gives no satisfactory explanation of the connection between the two. There is the same gap in a modern and equally well-known statement—that of the 1931 Primary School Report—that the curriculum is to be thought of in terms of experience rather than of 'knowledge to be acquired and facts to be stored' (paragraph 75). Clearly here the 'knowledge and facts' are thought of as mere words with which 'real' experience is contrasted, but the previous paragraphs do not throw much light on what could be meant by 'real' experience. Certainly it is something

---

[1] Bacon, Francis, *Advancement of Learning*, 1.1.3.
[2] Comenius, J. .A, *Great Didactic*, Chapter XX, 10.
[3] Locke, John, *Essay Concerning Human Understanding*, Book 2.
[4] Rousseau, *Julie* or *La Nouvelle Héloïse*.

more than sensation. One aspect is a criticism of industrialisation which has 'gripped the life of the people' so that the 'real business of life' has become 'increasingly difficult'. From this fact (which is reminiscent of Rousseau's condemnation of city civilisation) the Report draws the conclusion that schools should help to 'strengthen and enlarge the instinctive hold of children on the conditions of life by enriching, illuminating and giving point to their growing experience. The schools whose first intention was to teach children how to read have been compelled to broaden their aims until it might now be said that they have to teach children how to live' (paragraph 74). This is heady stuff but there is another line of attack in the Report, using A. N. Whitehead's criticism of 'inert' ideas as the Aunt Sally: 'No good can come from teaching children things that have no immediate value for them, however highly their potential or prospective value may be estimated. To put the point in a more concrete way, we must recognize the uselessness and danger of seeking to inculcate what Professor A. N. Whitehead calls inert ideas—that is, ideas which at the time when they are imparted have no bearing upon a child's natural activities of body or mind and do nothing to illuminate or guide his experiences' (paragraph 74). In fact this is not exactly what Whitehead meant because his definition of inert ideas was those which are 'merely received into the mind without being utilised or tested, or thrown into fresh combinations'.[5] However, he is with the authors of the Report in emphasising the importance of the present and of Life with a capital letter: 'There is only one subject-matter for education, and that is Life in all its manifestations'.[6]

This emphasis on 'living' as opposed to 'fact learning' is characteristic of many progressive educationalists. For instance, W. H. Kilpatrick contrasts the 'old curriculum' which consisted of 'systematically arranged content of knowledge to be acquired' with the 'new curriculum' which seeks 'as its immediate aim the highest and finest quality of living . . . relying on the fact that if children do really live this quality of life they will in that degree build the same quality of character'.[7]

But can one measure the 'quality of life' or the richness of experience? An experience which to one man may seem trivial will to another be full of significance. Emphasis on experience as the key to education can only make sense if we interpret it in terms of what goes on in the mind. It is not enough that a child's body should be active or that he should be manipulating his environment or that he should

[5] Whitehead, A. N., *Aims of Education* (Macmillan, 1929), p. 1.
[6] *Ibid.*, p. 7.
[7] Kilpatrick, W. H., *Philosophy of Education* (Macmillan, N.Y., 1951), p. 314.

be stimulated or even that he should be happy. The point at issue is not what he is doing viewed externally, but what is happening inside his mind. Unfortunately we have no means of finding that out. All we know, and we know that by inference, is that the quality of experience varies infinitely.

EXPERIENCE AS PERCEPTION

But let us get back from 'total living' to sense experience. From birth onward we are constantly receiving sensations through one or other of our senses, but sensation is not necessarily perception. Sensation is the nether limit of perception. Perception is when, taking a sensation as a cue, we see a thing for what it is, i.e. we recognise it as, say, a bicycle or an old lady or excessive speed. Most of our perception is done unhesitatingly. When we perceive something as being different or as something we are not quite sure of, we reflect and make a judgement. This is the upper limit of sensation. We could say that through our senses we receive certain data, on the basis of which we perceive or judge a thing to be such and such. Thus the sensation of blue comes to the eye as a certain wavelength of light. It is transmitted to the brain by impulses which are not blue or any other colour but we perceive it as blue. How we do so, how indeed we have any idea of colour as such, is a mystery. How the baby passes, in William James's striking language, from being 'assailed by eyes, ears, nose, skin and entrails at once, feeling it all as one great blooming, buzzing confusion' to the 'stream of consciousness' which is the normal condition of life, not even a fond mother, let alone a psychologist, can tell. It is *as if* from the beginning we had a vague idea what it was all about and gradually fitted the pieces of the jig-saw together.

Though we cannot understand the process we can describe certain aspects of it which are vital to our understanding of what is involved in experience. The first aspect is classification, which means picking out a thing as being 'of a kind'. We distinguish a thing from its background, then we identify it as something we know, then we classify it as an instance of what we already know; and these three processes occur together and are all part of what we mean by classi-fication. We may sense an infinity of things but we only perceive those we attend to, and this means we classify them. Unless we had some expectation or readiness to classify what we sense we could perceive nothing. In a very vague and tenuous way we must know what it is we see before we see it, otherwise we could not see it at all. There is more than a half-truth in saying that the child attends to what he wants to perceive. Indeed, we could go further and say that he makes objects conform to what he wants them to be. Thus, he sees a shape appearing at the end of the road but because he is looking for his father he sees the shape as his father. His perception is not, therefore, based on sense data so much as on inference from sense data.

Classification involves the perception of points of similarity between two things which are dissimilar. Thus a familiar object may exhibit many different appearances—back and fore, in the light and in the dark, alone and in a crowd—but we recognise that it is the same object. Or an object may be different from another, except in one property which we regard as essential to that category, and so we put them both into the same class. Often, of course, there is confusion. Is a pebble in the same class as a nut? Is a Shetland pony in the same class as a donkey?

The second aspect of the process of perception is language. There would be much more difficulty in classifying if, each time we had sense experience of a thing, we had to recollect other things with which it might be grouped and put them into the same class. It is often supposed that a baby's first perception is that of his mother, though she must appear to him in many different guises—bending low over him or approaching from a distance; as a face, a whole body or perhaps only as a breast; early in the morning or late at night; smiling or sad. His perception may be described as the fitting together of a 'standard' view, of which all the variations have common factors. But the process of giving unity and continuity to a world in which everything is in a state of flux is enormously helped by language. When the baby learns to say, 'Mum, mum', the word gives a kind of anchor to the floating idea. The act of expressing a percept fixes and distinguishes it finally. The young child loves to show his mastery of his environment by naming the things he perceives in it. Thus language is not an alternative to experience, nor even a desirable follow-up to it, but an essential part of it. It frees the child from the bondage of sensation because with its aid he not only recognises a thing in unfamiliar positions but, more important, he can summon up the idea of the thing even when it is not present to his senses. The phenomenal speed with which little children learn to speak is evidence of the fact that naming enables them to bring some sort of order into the mass of incidentals in which particulars are enmeshed. The word gives control of the thing. It facilitates the process of perceiving because it defines the thing permanently. Complaints about verbalism are only justified when words are divorced from sense experience. That is when ideas become inert. But language itself is not inert, on the contrary, it is the main means by which *homo sapiens* develops particular ideas into general ones.

Furthermore, language is the supreme link between minds. As human beings ascend from the sensation level to the perceptual level, and from that to the abstract level, they depend more and more on language. Language puts into our hands the key to common ideas and therefore makes possible common action.

Much of the progressive literature on education is confused on the relationship between the concrete and the abstract, but they cannot ever be separated without losing the significance of both. From the very beginning of life the concrete and the abstract are interlocked and language is the chief means by which this is brought about.

PERCEPTION IN THE CLASSROOM

A great deal of the work done in infant and lower junior schools might be described as providing experiences leading to increased perception. This may be considered under four headings:

1. *Collecting* At an early age children start collecting for themselves, and this means that they must be able to distinguish properties such as colour, shape, size, texture and number and, on this basis, put dissimilar things into classes. According to Piaget's account of development, this comes in the intuitive stage from $4\frac{1}{2}$ to 7 years. This natural impulse can be strengthened and refined by the teacher in many ways. She can encourage children to collect objects for an 'interest table' of, for instance, sea-shells or nuts or fruits. She can make a 'colour corner' to which children bring all the things they can find of a particular colour, and then the objects can be further divided according to shade of colour or texture or shape. The 'book corner' provides many opportunities for sorting out books into categories, such as books about animals, about the country, about hobbies etc. Sorting things out is a kind of tidying-up and this can be applied to the store cupboard or any other part of the room where things need 'putting in place'. The 'nature table' is another chance for classifying; it should not be allowed to become a motley heap of leaves, flowers, twigs, stones, nuts etc. The private collecting habits of children themselves vary according to age, sex, neighbourhood and current fashion but they can be encouraged in school. Finally, there is the collecting of information about such things as birthdays, pets, size of family, or the weather, and this can be used as a basis for setting.

2. *Displaying* This is an important part of perception because it means to arrange things in such a way that their meaning is made clear. Display focuses attention and teachers might do well to take

note of the art of the window-dresser whose aim is to catch the eye of the passer-by. There is always a danger in encouraging collecting in that the classroom will become so cluttered that nothing is noticeable, and to avoid this there must be frequent changing of the scene. Children very quickly become so accustomed to a collection of things that they cease to perceive them. 'Object lessons' in which something was prominently displayed for all to see and examine were once popular and this technique can still be used.

Pictures of things are a little further removed from reality than the actual three-dimensional object, but they have the advantage of showing a thing in its natural setting and of emphasising what is important. The televised or ciné picture has the additional attraction of movement. The danger is, of course, that the child may become so interested in detail that he does not go on to perceive new points of interest. He sees only the surface not the meaning. For older children the answer to this problem may be the diagram. John Adams, a pioneer at the beginning of the century, says on this matter, 'The place of the picture is at the beginning and end of the process of teaching . . . all between is the domain of the diagram'.[8] His argument is that at first a child needs something to catch his attention, something concrete and as near to reality as possible, but then he needs help in perceiving the relationships of parts to the whole and that this is best conveyed through a diagram. Finally he needs to be referred back to the real situation to see the thing in action. The temptation for the teacher is that of making the diagram a substitute for, and not a supplement to, reality.

It is normal for a project or centre of interest to be concluded with a visual display in which all that has been learnt is brought together. Often a frieze is the most convenient and attractive way of doing this, and it has the advantage that both individuals and groups can contribute to the final unity. If, however, a number of illustrations are put up separately it is well to see that they are so arranged that they point to a theme. A wall crowded with pictures and diagrams conveys no message and may be a waste of time. Focusing attention is the operative aim.

Children should be encouraged to make their illustrative work an aid to perception not an exercise in copying. For instance, they can draw things from unfamiliar angles, for example, as seen under a microscope, upside-down or back to front, stretched out or compressed, as seen by a fly, or in part. A good exercise in display as an aid to perception is to construct a catalogue of objects suitably illustrated. The underlying purpose of putting children's work up on

[8] Adams, John, *Exposition and Illustration in Teaching* (Macmillan, 1913), p. 350.

the wall is not as a reward for good work but rather as an exercise in displaying an idea to others.

3. *Defining* At every stage the word and the thing should be closely linked. The word by which a thing is known is its definition and as a general rule it can be said that nothing should be displayed without its appropriate label. As far as possible this labelling should be done by the children themselves, especially on colour, nature or interest tables. If a project display needs somewhat more elaborate sign-posting it is essential that the teacher should only display lettering which is both readable from a distance and a model for children's own labelling.

Many games can be invented involving description and definition, for example, guessing games based on descriptions of familiar objects or on description of their parts; following out verbal instructions (as in individual intelligence tests); dictionary games, such as inviting children to make their own dictionary of cookery or gardening.

Finding the right title for anything that is done is a big help towards perception. The 'right' title means not only accuracy but also pungency, and even humour on occasions. For instance, a walk through the woods could be followed by gathering together into a class-book descriptions of what was found and entitling the whole, 'Discovered in the wood, 3rd October'. The covers of printed books often give ideas of display which can be used for the title page of group booklets.

There is little danger that 'mere' words will become a substitute for reality if the two are always linked together. This habit has many incidental advantages as well, such as helping reading and vocabulary. For instance, the building up of a 'class museum' offers opportunities for accurate description in labels, captions, guides and catalogues.

4. *Conceptualising* It may be, as Piaget says, that conceptualising is not possible before there has been a stage of concrete operations, but this makes it all the more necessary that the concrete operations should be meaningful. This, in turn, may involve the construction of apparatus specially designed to aid conceptualising, like the Montessori apparatus which was carefully designed to develop perception. A more modern example is the mathematical apparatus which is now common in primary schools, two types of which are described here. Cuisenaire rods consist of a set of coloured wooden rods of square cross-section. There are ten lengths, from one to ten centimetres, each having a distinctive colour and each representing a number. The purpose is to demonstrate abstract concepts such as

addition or subtraction by getting the child to manipulate the rods. In the colour-factor set the intention is the same but there is an additional concept demonstrated, i.e. that of prime factors. Thus the unit rod is white, and the three smallest prime numbers are represented by the three primary colours: red, blue and yellow. The higher numbers are coloured according to their factors, for example since $8 = 1 \times 2 \times 2 \times 2$ the 8-rod is coloured maroon, i.e. a triple power of 2. There are twelve rods of one centimetre in the set so that the concept of factors can be easily demonstrated. In similar fashion the Dienes apparatus demonstrates the principle of bases, while Stern and Unifix demonstrate the structure of numbers. However it would be misleading to suggest that by concrete operations children will always gain the concepts which we, as adults, think they should. Although we may have abstract ideas we do not obtain them each time from particular actions; on the other hand action frequently repeated will eventually be assimilated and become conceptual.

An example of the difference of point of view between the child and the adult may be found in an investigation which Piaget made into the 'why' questions of children. The adult thinks that to ask 'why' such and such a thing happened is an indication of concern for causality. But Piaget found that the majority of children's 'why' questions are concerned with living or moving things with which they could identify themselves. He concluded that the main purpose of the questions was not so much curiosity about causality as identification of the self with something in the external world.[9]

Again to refer to Piaget, in the matter of moral development we must be aware of the fallacy of putting old heads on young shoulders. It takes time for the child to develop the moral concept of reciprocal respect between persons and therefore his idea of 'fairness' may be different from the teacher's. Thus the teacher's sense of justice may be misconstrued by children whose ideas on the subject are still at the egocentric or authoritarian stage of development. If, however, children are encouraged to discuss moral questions freely, and even to act out their mistaken ideas, they may come to a rational and abstract concept of justice.[10] A. S. Neill claimed that his weekly meeting of the school at which social and moral matters were discussed was 'of more value than a week's curriculum of school subjects', even though sometimes the decisions seemed arbitrary or even harsh.[11]

[9] Piaget, Jean, *The Language and Thought of the Child* (Routledge & Kegan Paul 1926), pp. 165–198.

[10] See Piaget, Jean, *Moral Judgement of the Child* (Routledge & Kegan Paul, 1932).

[11] Neill, A. S., *Talking of Summerhill* (Gollancz, 1967), pp. 31–4.

LEARNING BY EXPERIENCE

The phrase 'learning by experience' is a common one but it is used with different shades of meaning. The emphasis can be on learning by doing rather than by theorising; or it can be on practice rather than on a few performances, however successful. The experienced person is thought to exercise his skill automatically. Or again, the emphasis can be on the constructive response to making mistakes as when we speak of 'trial and error' learning. Here the question at issue is whether the learner does in fact learn from his mistakes how to correct them, although it is certain that once he has begun to eliminate failure he begins to develop self-confidence and understanding for the difficulties of others. We think of an experienced man as one who is not anxious about his own performance nor intolerant of the efforts of others. He 'keeps his head'.

However, the meaning of learning by experience which we shall consider is the one taken by John Dewey that the two are synonymous. Both learning and experience may be taken as indicating a change of behaviour or conditions brought about by the interaction of an individual and his environment. From the learner's point of view there is a problem arising from environment and the change of conditions is his solution to the problem. From the point of view of the environment conditions impinge on the learner causing him to modify his behaviour. The same argument may be found in Piaget's terms accommodation and assimilation. Thus Dewey says:

'The nature of experience is understood only by noting that it includes an active and a passive element peculiarly combined. On the active side, experience is trying—a meaning which is made explicit in the connected term experiment. On the passive it is undergoing. When we experience something we act upon it, we do something with it; then we suffer or undergo the consequences. We do something to the thing and then it does something to us in return. . . . When activity is continued into the undergoing of consequences, the mere flux is loaded with significance. We learn something. It is not experience when a child sticks his finger into a flame; it is experience when the movement is connected with the pain which he undergoes in consequence.'[12]

Clearly, the extent to which experience is synonymous with learning determines the quality of the experience. To quote Dewey again, 'the measure of the value of an experience lies in the perception of

[12] Dewey, John, *Democracy and Education* (Collier Macmillan, 1916; Free Press Edn., 1966), pp. 139–40.

relationships or continuities to which it leads up. It includes cognition to the degree in which it is cumulative or amounts to something or has meaning'.[13] So, to have an experience is to learn something and, equally, to learn something is to have a resulting experience. We cannot separate the one from the other.

However, John Hanson, in an article entitled *Learning by Experiences* is critical of Dewey's line of thought as an educational principle. He quotes some remarks of Tom Sawyer: 'I can tell you, Jim, Uncle Abner was down on them people that's all the time trying to dig a lesson out of everything that happens, no matter whether . . .'[14] The problem is that the same experience, viewed externally, can have diametrically opposite effects on two people. One person will react to failure by 'learning' to avoid that kind of situation, another will be challenged by it to greater effort. Suffering will make one man sensitive to the pain of others and another hard and self-protective. Whatever may be the 'quality' in Dewey's terms of an experience, unexpected by-products will come in. Thus we cannot, with any certainty of success, plan a programme of experiences designed to produce the kind of learning we value, nor is an experience an automatic or inevitable product of the interaction of the individual and environment. There are too many ambiguities in the phrase 'learning by experience' to warrant its acceptance as a principle of method. Hanson concludes, 'Certainly "learning by experience" gives us no cues as to which types of product have ensued . . . and no genuinely applicable standard of evaluation to employ in judging whether the learning thus secured is to be valued. Thus we are brought back to Tom Sawyer's distinction between experiences which do "educate a person" and "the forty million lots of the other kind"'.[15]

However, Dewey is on firmer ground in his argument that the experience of problem-solving is typical of scientific method. His outline of the procedures of science is accurate enough and of much relevance to teaching: first the awareness of a problem in the environment, then the search for relevant data, then the formulation and testing of possible solutions, then selection of the most promising solution, and finally the subjecting of this hypothesis to rigorous validation. The process depends in origin upon a spirit of inquiry, an urge to discover, a refusal to choose blindly when faced with a 'fork in the road' situation. The *Plowden Report* gives two reasons for the heuristic approach to science, one positive and the other negative.

[13] *Ibid.*, p. 140.
[14] Mark Twain, *Tom Sawyer Abroad*.
[15] Hanson, John, 'Learning by Experience', in Smith, B. O. and Ennis, R. H., *Language and Concepts in Education* (Rand McNally, 1967), p. 20.

Positively, it speaks of the child's 'strong drive towards the exploration of his environment and about novel and unexpected features of his environment' (paragraph 45). Negatively, it declares that 'if primary science is confined to knowledge taken from books, the whole purpose of the study of this area of the curriculum will be lost' (paragraph 669).

For many years science teaching in the primary school was limited to nature study and it consisted for the most part of observation and recording of nature in the school locality, helped out by object lessons and a class textbook. Several factors have brought about a change in approach in the last ten years. Many new primary schools have been built on the open-plan with adequate practical work areas, but they are predominantly in cities, away from the rural environment which made the traditional nature study reasonable. There was a general movement of opinion in favour of more attention being given to science throughout the country, and, to meet the needs of teachers ill-equipped to teach science, the BBC began its 'Junior Science' series in 1961. Then many local authorities began to provide courses and resources in science, and in 1964 the Nuffield Foundation began the Junior Science Project.

The Project was remarkable for a number of things. First it represented a conscious attempt at innovation, with a complete shift from direct teaching to discovery methods in which the onus was put on the children. Then resources were made available so that the innovation might be led by a team of 'experts' in different parts of the country. At the same time, there was a total rejection of the idea that experts should provide pre-packaged teaching material; their function was to give advice and encouragement but not to spoon-feed teachers who felt inadequate. In any case it was hoped to get over the latter problem by concentrating on everyday things using simple apparatus and avoiding altogether the specialisation of the secondary schools. The function of the teacher was envisaged as that of helping children to find answers to their own questions and then to communicate their findings in their own way. Many teachers found it hard to do this. They could not accept the idea of non-directive teaching and felt that at least there must be an agreed scheme such as earth, air and water or the concepts of matter, relationship and change. Second, many teachers were disturbed to find that junior children did not communicate their findings in the conventional ways they were familiar with. While the support of the project team continued teachers remained enthusiastic but they tended to expect the kind of help which the team did not wish to give, i.e. study kits or sets of work cards. Teachers wanted to treat science as a subject on the timetable and to have schemes of work prepared, whereas the belief of the project team was that all children can, if encouraged, ask their own worthwhile questions and plan ways of finding answers to them. There are particular cases of teachers and schools ready to experiment and to explore with the children some of the puzzles of the environment which, in a scientific age, are matters of common discussion.[16]

LEARNING TO EXPERIENCE

No account of experience would be complete without consideration of feeling. This is a word with many shades of meaning. It has something to do with physical sensation since sights, sounds, odours, tastes and touch give pleasure or pain. It is closely associated with the emotions of hope, fear, love, hate, anger and despair. It is used particularly to describe affectionate relationships. It refers to awareness of the reactions of others or to sympathy for their experiences. It is used to express intuition or simply a state of consciousness in which there is dread or expectation. Since human beings are egocentric, feeling is concerned with the defence of the ego and consequently involves attack upon or withdrawal from whatever threatens it. Education is therefore concerned with the various ways in which strong feelings can be controlled, expressed or redirected; and learning to experience is acquiring the various ways which men have found for this end, whether cathartic, sublimatory, or purifying. When feeling is released and expressed there is an immediate relief of tension. The problem is to do this harmlessly, or constructively. Even scientific inquiry is sustained by the momentum of feeling.

During the course of evolution man has discovered various ways in which he can learn to experience. This is the basis of art. The artist is one who creates images which embody and convey his own feeling experiences. Even in the visual arts the image need not correspond closely to the original stimulus, while in music the image is in rhythm and melody and is non-representational. The appreciation of art is, therefore, a personal matter in which each individual gets from the artist whatever expression of his own feelings he can. For children the appreciation lesson is an experiment in feeling. The child will be unlikely to analyse the poem, picture or symphony intellectually but something of its spirit may seep into his consciousness and clarify or satisfy his feeling hunger. The teacher's function is to select what is most likely to appeal, to share the experience with his pupils, to create an atmosphere quietly receptive—and then to leave well alone. A child can be deeply moved by something he does

[16] Nuffield Science has been taken up with enthusiasm in Ontario, Canada recently.

not understand in full like 'the multitudinous seas incarnadine' or 'sounding brass or a clanging cymbal'. It is difficult to generalise where there is so much individual variation but the strongest argument in favour of the daily act of worship in schools is the opportunity it offers for giving a true feeling experience. Wonder, awe, thankfulness and reverence are basic to the human condition, and it is possible to create an atmosphere in which they can flourish although some children will, inevitably, be untouched.

Learning to experience has a receptive and an active side. We may consider the receptive aspect in relation to the *story*. The skill of story-telling in primary schools is unfortunately much neglected and, although it would be wrong to suggest that *reading* a story is necessarily inferior, narration has so much more scope for creating and responding to group feeling that it is a skill no primary teacher should neglect. In telling a story the teacher is not simply recounting what happened; he is also letting the children be vividly aware of his own participation in the feeling of it. Both teller and listener must share the cathartic experience and this is more difficult if one is tied to the printed page. It is the little 'asides', the dramatic gestures, the expressive eyes, the emotional pauses which make the good story-teller so marvellously able to hold the class 'in the hollow of his hand.' As to the choice of stories to tell, one should remember that the basic situation must 'speak to the condition' of individual children. They find the world a rare mixture of mystery and familiarity, of fearsome dangers and reassuring security. They frequently feel inadequate, powerless and dependent and yet conscious of powers within and without that can help them to triumph over hostile forces. They know what it is to be tempted to shirk duty, to hide under fantasy, to yield to self-pity. But they also have a natural optimism that things will turn out right in the end, and an instinctive belief in goodness finally reconciled. Therefore, stories must reflect these feeling experiences and it does not much matter whether they are about slum children, Greek heroes or spacemen so long as the children can identify themselves. The stories that appeal to children are basically timeless: David and Goliath, Hansel and Gretel, Jason and the Golden Fleece. Children can tolerate plenty of tension, even of sadness and tragedy, but they do want a happy ending. Somehow the ogres, the villains, the figures of harsh authority must be worsted or reconciled; otherwise the world is unbearable. Faced with this simple recipe for story-making there is no reason why imaginative teachers should not create their own stories, bearing in mind the particular emotional problems of individuals.

On the active side, art is that part of the primary curriculum which is specially adapted for the expression and relief of feeling. But 'art' now has a far wider meaning than drawing or painting. It is correlated with all art forms, using words, music or craft as well as pictorial representation. We can, however, distinguish two aspects: creativity and self-expression. On the creative side the child is fulfilling an artistic function in decorating something or making a stimulating environment. This applies to all the 'pattern-making' activities whether using colour as such or sticking on seeds, pebbles, pieces of paper, glass or leaves. Then creative work can be done with all sorts of improvised or junk material such as branches, roots, twigs, bark, clay impressions, etc. Almost anything which is not dangerous to handle (for example, tin cans) can be brought into service as the raw material from which some pleasing shape can be created. In recent years there has been a great development of the art of 'collage' which approaches three-dimensional forms by using scraps of dress and furnishing textiles embellished by such oddments as fur, beads, buttons or ribbon. So far as feeling experience is concerned the important contribution of what may be called 'mosaic' art is that in becoming absorbed in it the child is incidentally relieved of tension.

Art is, however, also a means of expressing specific feeling and of symbolising experience. As this is inevitably highly personal it is difficult to evaluate in objective terms but many teachers are coming to realise that they had underestimated the art ability of children. Their basic taste is good though they often fall into conventional patterns which become banal and repetitive. The teacher needs also to watch for the times when the child can be helped to acquire a new technique and, on occasion, to provide the stimuli which will spark off self-expression.

It would, however, be a pity if the recent enthusiasm for pattern-making and self-expression implied that representational art had no place in school. On the contrary, the forms of nature are a constant source of inspiration.

FURTHER READING

Blackwell, F. F., *Starting Points for Science* (Blackwell, 1968).

Centre for Curriculum Renewal and Educational Development Overseas, *Children at School, Primary Education in Britain Today* (Heinemann, 1969).

Dean, Joan, *A Place to Paint* (Evans, 1972).

Dewey, John, *Experience and Education* (Collier Macmillan, 1938).

Dewey, John, *Art as Experience* (Minton Balch, 1934).

Dewey, John, *Experience and Nature* (Open Court Publishing Co., Chicago, 1925).

Foster, John, *Discovery Learning in the Primary School* (Macmillan, 1972).

Foster, John, *Creativity and the Teacher* (Macmillan, 1972).

Grugeon, David, *An Infants School* (Macmillan, 1971).

Hanson, John, 'Learning by Experience', in Smith, B. O., and Ennis, R. H., *Language and Concepts in Education* (Rand McNally, 1967).

Heydebrand, Caroline, *Childhood, A Study of the Growing Soul* (Rudolf Steiner Press, Revised Ed., 1970).

Hudgins, Bryce, *Problem Solving in the Classroom* (Macmillan, 1966).

Jameson, K., *Pre-school and Infant Art* (Evans, 1968).

Jenkins, Mollie, *School without Tears* (Collins, 1973).

Jones, R. M., *Fantasy and Feeling in Education* (Penguin, 1972).

Langer, Suzanne, *Feeling and Form* (Harvard Univ. Press, 1953).

Lee, Doris M. and Allen, R. V., *Learning to Read Through Experience* (Appleton Century, 1963).

Lewis, Francis, *And Softly Tread* (A. & C. Black, 1971).

Longley, Peter, *Discovering Religion* (Lutterworth Press, 1971).

Lytton, Hugh, *Creativity and Education* (Routledge & Kegan Paul, 1971).

Mabey, Richard, *Children in the Primary School. The Learning Experience* (Penguin, 1972).

Marshall, Sybil, *Experiment in Education* (CUP, 1963).

Marshall, Sybil, *Aspects of Art Work* (Evans, 1967).

McKellar, P., *Imagination and Thinking* (Cohen & West, 1957).

Melzi, May, *Art in the Primary School* (Blackwell, 1967).

Moch, Ruth, *Education and the Imagination* (Chatto & Windus, 1970).

Nuffield Junior Science Project, *Teacher's Guide 1; Teacher's Guide 2; Source Book; Apparatus, Source Book; Animals & Plants* (Collins, 1967).

Pluckrose, Henry, *Picture Making with Juniors* (Oldbourne, 1968).

Pluckrose, Henry, *Art* (Macmillan, 1972).

Probert, Howard and Jarman, Christopher, *A Junior School* (Macmillan, 1971).

Pullan, J. M., *Towards Informality* (Macmillan, 1971).

Reid, Louis Arnaud, *Ways of Knowledge and Experience* (Heinemann, 1961).

Spodek, Bernard, *Teaching in the Early Years* (Prentice Hall, 1972).

Stauffen, Russell G., *Reading, A Thinking Process* (Harper & Row, 1969).

Tomlinson, R. R., *Children as Artists* (Penguin, 1944).

Victor, Edward, *Science for the Elementary School* (Collier Macmillan, 1970).

Weber, Lillian, *The English Infants School and Informal Education* (Prentice Hall, 1971).

Yardley, Alice, *Discovering the Physical World* (Evans, 1970).

Yardley, Alice, *Senses and Sensitivity* (Evans, 1970).

Yardley, Alice, *The Teacher of Young Children* (Evans, 1971).

Chapter 6

Activity

MEANINGS OF 'ACTIVITY' IN EDUCATION

'Activity' is an emotive word among primary teachers. Few would disclaim support for it and practically all infant teachers would claim to be practising it. Junior teachers are not so unanimous. Their hesitation springs from two fears: first, that it may threaten law and order, than which nothing to them is more important; and second, that basic skills may suffer. The abandoning of 11-plus selection has lessened the shadow of competition; whether the new three-tier system will draw the middle school more into line with the secondary, or whether it will bring an extension upward of the infant school ethos is hard to say at this time. The design of new schools is a factor favouring activity methods because it gives more space, and more flexibility with what space there is. The *Plowden Report* gave the stamp of official approval to what is known as the 'activity' principle. On the other hand, a good many earnest teachers are uneasy because they realise that physical movement by itself is no certain indication of mental movement. The child who moves about aimlessly or performs a practical manipulation without thought may well be wasting his time. This is the worry that gnaws at the conscience of many conscientious teachers.

Partly the problem is one of definition. If we look back to a book which was very popular with students twenty-five years ago: M. V. Daniel's *Activity in the Primary School* (1948), we find a variety of meanings given. She speaks of the 'great vigour and activity shown by children during this period', of the 'concrete basis needed for the early stages of reasoning', and of the need for 'direct contact with the child's world inside and outside the school boundaries'.[1] She warns teachers of the fallacy of treating activity as a subject of the curriculum (some do in fact put 'activities' as a timetabled subject) since it is a method of approach to education which permeates every subject and all sides of school life. It can begin from any one subject of the curriculum, and, as an example, she mentions the case of a class 'which became interested in stories from the Old Testament and

[1] Daniel, M. V., *Activity in the Primary School* (Blackwell, 1948), pp. 50–1.

extended the work to art, composition, play-writing and a number of other activities'.[2] She goes on to discuss certain limitations of the activity approach saying that 'active' periods do not provide the right conditions for acquiring mechanical skills. It is only through constant practice that fluency is gained in reading; an easy, quick style is acquired in writing and speed, and accuracy is reached in simple arithmetical operations. The study of a subject or topic along activity lines provides the incentive and the opportunity to use these tools, but it is only with practice that skill is attained and definite lessons should be planned for this purpose. Then she continues, 'A more formal approach is needed in other aspects of Primary work. The knowledge children acquire through the study of different topics is incomplete and unorganized. This knowledge must be drawn together and reduced to order in a set lesson.'[3]

So much for what a pioneer thought on the subject. Since then, progress has been made in discovering new shades of meaning and new emphases, of which the following may be mentioned:

1. The possibility for greater physical movement has been greatly increased by open-plan schools in which several classes share a large work area, by open-plan classrooms in which a conventional room is partitioned-off into special interest areas, and by opening the classroom doors so that children can go to the library or work in the corridor or use any spare space available in the school. This does not mean that sitting still is educationally unsound but that it becomes so if made compulsory over long periods.

2. The keynote of activity methods has come to be their informality. This means that there is no set pattern, no pre-determined plan, no common procedure which all must follow. Instead, there is much more improvisation by the teacher; he takes advantage of suggestions from children and if he makes plans he modifies them freely. Among the children there is much more variation between one and another; each develops at his own pace and in his own way. Individual differences are allowed and encouraged. At the same time group co-operation is stimulated as much as possible because this means that children learn from each other.

3. There has been a movement away from the idea that activities spring from 'subjects' because the very concept of a timetable is being challenged. The integrated day opens the way for an almost unlimited range of choice, the only limiting factor being the resources available. Then there has been a challenge to the class-teacher system, and various forms of team teaching are being introduced which

[2] *Ibid.*, p. 54.
[3] *Ibid.*, p. 62.

means that there can be great flexibility in what is done. This comparative looseness of organisation has its dangers as the best primary teachers readily acknowledge; they say that their biggest problem is to keep track of what each individual child is doing and to ensure that what he is doing is worthwhile. Teachers who practise activity methods with enthusiasm get great satisfaction from watching and sharing the children's spontaneous interests, but they have to be constantly on the alert to ensure that individuals are not falling by the wayside. It may well be that the only answer to this problem with large classes is to use 'kits' on likely topics so that any child who is 'at a dead end' can be given something simple and yet stimulating to do.

4. Activity methods, as now practised, imply a different kind of school situation from the traditional one. It is envisaged that parents and people outside the school staff will be drawn in, as is mentioned in the *Plowden Report*. It is also felt that school must be thought of more as a base from which operations in the locality can be planned, than as a place of detention to which children are sent for so many hours a day. In addition, school work is to be considered as a social service, either for the benefit of the school or of the neighbourhood. Ultimately it is hoped, by some far-seeing people, that community schools, in the best sense of the word, will develop.

Finally it must be said that the activity approach is no primrose path to success. Some schools, some neighbourhoods, some teachers, and some children seem not to thrive on activity methods. The official *Report on Primary Education* of 1959 makes this point when it says, 'The fact is that all teachers are not gifted enough to improvise profitably, that all children are not culturally prepared to use their own initiative and that all schools are not equipped to make free movement possible'.[4]

THEORETICAL BASIS OF ACTIVITY IN EDUCATION

To make a success of activity methods one must at least believe in them. But on what grounds? Shall it be a romantic idealism concerning the innate goodness of the child despite all evidence to the contrary? Or shall it be a conviction about the nature of truth that it involves a constant search? Or shall it be based on a theory of human development that all understanding arises from doing? Each of these arguments has had its advocates and each of them has a germ of truth. Let us look at them in turn.

The case for romantic idealism was put most eloquently by Rousseau in the opening pages of *Emile*. He begins, 'God makes all things good.' Therefore, in appealing to nature as the foundation of all education he was on firm ground. But what is nature? Rousseau

[4] *Primary Education* (HMSO, 1959), p. 52.

defines it as the 'innate disposition' and 'inner growth of our organs and faculties'. Granted this premise, it follows that the 'natural' activities of children are the conditions of emergent growth and that they are, in fact, conditions of learning. Learning is not simply a function of mind, but of the 'whole' of the child's nature—body, mind and spirit. But Rousseau went a stage further. He argued that these 'natural' activities take place in a 'natural' environment, i.e. not the artificial urban environment created by man. Thus he says, 'You must make your choice between the man and the citizen, you cannot train both.'

Pestalozzi was deeply impressed by *Emile* but he recognised that all children could not have a private tutor. He was concerned for the education of the poor. To this problem he devoted his attention and his life, and his conclusion was that education must take the good peasant home as its model. For instance, 'There can be no doubt that within the living room of every household are united the essential basic elements of all true human education in its whole range.'[5] Thus, the activities which should be included in school education were to be as near as possible to those which a child would perform in a good home, however poor it might be. 'Nature', for Pestalozzi, was the intuition of the mother; and this was the key to educational method because the mother taught instinctively. As he says, 'Indeed the existence and the unity of the method reveals itself nowhere so purely and so sublimely as in the way either the completely trained mother or the quite simple, natural mother treats her child. Her treatment is elemental, it is distorted by no human confusion; in it nature expresses her whole self.'[6]

'Nature' was given a further shade of meaning by Froebel, different from the child-centredness of Rousseau or the mother-centredness of Pestalozzi. For Froebel, the centre was God. To describe the activities necessary in education he frequently uses the word 'representation'. Human life should be a 'representation of the divine nature within'. Children should be taught to make things which represent ideas of divine origin. Men's work is done in partnership with God and children, in imitating their elders, are repeating the process. This exalted interpretation of activities is not peculiar to Froebel; it was strong in Comenius in the seventeenth century and it is repeated in Rudolf Steiner in the twentieth century. Undoubtedly it is a faith which sustains teachers in dealing with maladjusted and handicapped children as much as with normal wayward and difficult ones. Especially for the child up to the age of

[5] Pestalozzi, *Schriften* 4, p. 475.
[6] *Ibid.*, p. 182.

7, the education provided in a Steiner school is intended to build up his soul by imitation and physical activity. The purpose of the painting, drawing, modelling, acting, eurythmy, singing, and learning poems is to build up spiritual consciousness. The child is thought of as a living witness to God.

Many teachers will feel unable to subscribe to romantic idealism in any of its forms as a sufficient basis for activity methods. They would rather take their stand on the nature of truth, and they will take this not in any high philosophic sense but as realistically as possible. To the pragmatist, the truth of a statement is simply its workability. This bald definition could be made more explicit by saying that the crucial test of whether an idea is true or not is its long-range effectiveness in the conquest of difficulties. Therefore the search for truth is an endeavour to bring about desirable change in the environment. The word 'environment' is used here in a wide sense, to indicate social and cultural factors as well as physical ones. The environment is, so to speak, the anvil on which activity works.

What are the implications for activity methods of this theory of truth? The first is that in a simple rural environment many of the conditions would be found for educative activities if the members of that community would consciously direct their efforts to helping children. Unfortunately many fail to do so; hence the need for schools. In any case, in an industrialised society most children are in an unfavourable environment; hence again the need for schools. But, as John Dewey says, 'it is not the business of the school to transport youth from an environment of activity into one of cramped study of the records of other men's learning; but to transport them from an environment of relatively chance activities into one of activities selected with reference to guidance of learning.'[7] So, therefore, a school is an experimental environment designed to foster the search for truth in the pragmatic sense. It was to be a 'kind of laboratory for the discovery of the conditions under which labour may become intellectually fruitful and not merely externally productive'.[8] This was Dewey's answer to the criticism that pragmatic education was narrowly utilitarian. The activities of the experimental school are only utilitarian in the sense that they are directed towards solving problems that are seen by the people concerned, teachers and children, to be relevant to their situation. They are only artificial in the sense that they are designed for a specific purpose. Dewey says, 'Schools remain the typical instance of environments framed with express reference to influencing the mental and moral dispositions

[7] Dewey, John, *Democracy and Education* (Free Press Edn, 1968, First published by the Macmillan Co., 1916), p. 274.
[8] *Ibid.*, p. 275.

of their members.'[9] A further development of the idea of a laboratory school is that of the community school, where the surrounding natural-social environment is used as the stimulus for activities consistent with a search for truth.

Certain weaknesses in the pragmatic argument are apparent. How can anyone tell the 'long-range effectiveness' of a solution to a problem? How long-range? In any case, can we expect children to feel that long-range effectiveness is relevant to them? Furthermore, can the school provide an environment which is not far more artificial than the pragmatists would admit? In it the children are protected from the problems of the everyday world and the problems which are presented to them are inevitably pseudo-problems, in the sense that they serve no obvious purpose. Thus, for instance, in a book with the title *Pragmatism in Education* the author gives as a typical example of problem-raising the question: When was America discovered and by whom? This may be an interesting problem but can hardly be said to arise out of an environment.[10]

Is it not, therefore, more feasible to think in terms of a theory of human development and make this the basis for the activities of the primary school? The theory which has had most influence in recent years in this matter is that of Piaget, and so we will look briefly at his main principles. Piaget begins with the idea that thought is assimilated action. On the basis of concrete experiences we build mental 'schemas', i.e. mental frameworks within which we make sense of the world. Now the building up of these frameworks takes time and goes through stages spread over the first twelve years or so of life. Each stage has its appropriate type of activity which cannot be by-passed and has to come to a state of equilibrium before the next stage can come about. According to Piaget even the most elaborate environment cannot accelerate mental development very far in advance of biological maturation. The particular character of the primary school stage arises from the fact that concrete operations precede any level of abstract thinking. This gives us at once a good reason for giving children in the primary school abundance of practical activity and a cue for deciding what are the most significant forms of that activity.

The kind of 'concrete operations' which we must use are such as will demonstrate thought processes possible for an adult in an abstract form but not possible for a child of primary age. Take, for instance, the concept of conservation. Adults have little trouble in tracing a physical operation back to its starting point *in their minds* and, therefore, of realising that the particular elements may change

[9] *Ibid.*, p. 19.
[10] Bayles, Ernest E., *Pragmatism in Education* (Harper & Row, 1966), p. 82.

but that amount, weight, volume or size will remain the same. In Piaget's terms they can reverse a physical operation mentally. For the child, it is difficult to imagine *possible* relations among objects present to the senses, still less to manipulate possible relations among absent objects. He has to learn how to perceive aspects of his environment as invariant, despite the fact that his senses tell him they are always changing. The function of school is to facilitate, and accelerate if it can, the stage of concrete operations by providing those activities in which logical operations are demonstrated. This applies particularly in mathematics, but has applications also in science.

The argument in favour of activities because of a theory of human development may also be supported in the case of Gandhi. When Indian independence became imminent, Gandhi turned his mind to the Indian educational system which he found deficient in almost every respect. It was bookish and European in outlook and totally inappropriate to the needs of the majority of people, who were villagers. At the same time, Gandhi was completely against the idea that there should be two kinds of education, rural and urban, because the great need of city dwellers was to have more direct contact with the land and with crafts.

So the programme which Gandhi proposed for education was that manual work should be the basis for three or four hours per day and that the training of the mind should stem from this. The central craft which he recommended was that of spinning because, firstly, the spinning wheel or *charkha* was cheap, traditional, and simple enough for children to manipulate; second that it was a good example of what he called 'bread labour', i.e. labour which had a useful economic function; and third, because spinning yarn involved other processes such as ginning, carding and slivering and led on to weaving, all of which could be performed with skill. Not that the craft of making clothes was the only basic craft. Gandhi was deeply concerned that all people should grow up with first-hand experience of agriculture and with their roots firmly in the land. Production and preparation of food was obviously a basic craft.

Gandhi was aware of the fact that mechanical labour is not, in itself, educative and that children's labour might well be exploited. Therefore he argued that mental powers of inquiry and research must find scope for development through craft. He also said that craft must be communal, with teacher and children joining in service to the community, i.e. he urged the community school. Vinoba Bhave, who may be looked upon as the leading interpreter of 'basic education', says on this point, 'Teacher and pupil will take part as occasion arises in village cleaning and other public service; the teacher should habitually work with the pupils in sweeping and cleaning the school, plastering the courtyard with cow-dung etc. Such so-called "low" kinds of work must not be put upon the children; the teacher must first do them himself and then get the children to take part'.[11] Though craft was to form the basis of Gandhian education, intellectual and spiritual values were not to be neglected, and work and knowledge were never to be separated. Vinoba gives the following list of essential areas of knowledge which all children should have: facility in speech; knowledge of great poems by heart; discussion of the ideas of Gandhian philosophy; and the basic concepts of science and the laws of health, nutrition, hygiene, cookery, etc.

Something along the lines of basic education has been tried in various parts of the Third World, either sponsored by UNESCO as, for instance, in the Philippines and Thailand; or by government as in Tanzania. But the schemes have had varying success and the reasons for lack of progress are not difficult to see, i.e. preoccupation with literacy; popular contempt for agriculture and manual labour; and, above all, the difficulty of finding teachers with enough vision to make craft-centred education a reality. Slowly, however, the idea is gaining ground that schools should be more open to the community than heretofore; more available for village betterment; more earthy in fact, with compost-making and latrine-construction taking precedence over fact-learning. It could be said that activity methods, in whatever form and in whatever situation, demand a vision as well as a methodology.

THE PLAY SPIRIT

That practical activities arising from the felt needs of a community are not inconsistent with pleasurable experience is behind the various attempts in Britain to create genuine community schools, as in the Liverpool area. Nevertheless it must be admitted that the spirit of play (as opposed to entertainment) is hard to achieve in an industrialised society. Although activities in school should not be purpose*less* there are other worthwhile purposes besides the utilitarian and immediate ones. The spirit of play, which is essentially non-serious, is indispensable for the period of childhood growth, and this is not inconsistent with the doctrine of Froebel that play is serious. Of course it is—but the seriousness is not of the kind that must distinguish adult work.

Play is accepted as a normal part of nursery and infant education but junior school teachers are somewhat ambivalent in their attitude towards it. They have the feeling that any activities must have some

[11] Vinoba Bhave, *Thoughts on Education* (Sarva Seva Sangh, 1959), p. 110.

connection, if not with the outside world, at least with the 'subjects' of secondary education. Play seems to have no objective beyond itself; it is its own justification. Their covert criticism of much of the play that goes on with younger children is that it is hard to distinguish from 'messing about'. All the emphasis is on the process and none on the product of the activity.

It is therefore necessary in any consideration of the concept of activity to discuss the criteria by which the spirit of play can be distinguished.

The first criterion by which the play spirit can be judged is that of the degree of imagination involved. To say that play represents an attempt to escape from the real world must not be interpreted to mean that it has nothing to do with reality. It is a restructuring of reality to make it more tolerable or interesting. Three examples will suffice to make this point. A sick child in bed tries to create a 'land of counterpane' in which his physical limitations can be forgotten. A little boy is 'playing bears' at home, and the hearth-rug is an ice-floe on which he is precariously balanced and beyond which is the open sea; the reality is the familiar furniture of his lounge but he has created another 'reality', that of an Arctic landscape. A little girl is playing at school in the Wendy House; she sees it as 'home' but, instead of being the dependent child, she is the mother caring for her baby and welcoming home her husband. In all these cases there is the element of make-believe, of day-dreaming, of fantasy, but the child is not deceived into thinking that this is reality except in so far as it is 'his' reality. Now he may do this with much or little imagination, but the essence of his situation is that he is supposing what his situation would be like *if* . . .

The second criterion of play is its freedom from external control; it is this which makes it pleasurable. The child can flit from one occupation to another without reprimand; he can choose *this* rather than *that*; and his activity is temporarily freed from the limitations of time and space and of his own inadequacy—but only temporarily, of course. A sudden spasm of pain brings to an abrupt end the land of counterpane; Mother announces that bed-time must put an end to playing bears; and interruptions to the Wendy House drama are inevitable. But for the present the child at play has the feeling of spontaneity. Even though the sequence may have been repeated a dozen times each one is unique, with unforeseeable possibilities. Each situation, however dull to the outsider, has the chance of new illumination. On the whole it is clear that adults lose the capacity which they had as children for intense spontaneity.

The third criterion is the social character of play. This may seem inconsistent, but although in practice play is so often solitary, imaginatively it is social. Frequently it is imitative, taking its cues from some real or imagined situation. Often it is conventional, for children take on the play habits of their siblings or friends. It does not arise in a social vacuum, and although with little children play is often individual, there comes a time when normally the child will need companions in his play. This redeems it from the futility of mere day-dreaming. Only children are peculiarly in need of companions in their play. It is true that very young children play *beside* other children, rather than with them, but even then the children influence one another and parallel play is an introduction to more highly developed social play. Thus, for instance, the three-year-old cannot be with others without learning to 'take turns' and share toys or room space. This accommodation of others may be regarded as the beginnings of the acceptance of rules in games, and as providing an introduction to group co-operation and group competition. Awareness of the 'other' is important in relation to sex. Although normally boys and girls of primary school age play separately, the primary school is essentially a co-educational institution in which each sex becomes aware of the characteristics of the other. In a desire to make groups sociometric we should not do anything to prevent the shifting of play groups. At the present time there is considerable public interest in the provision of educational play for the under-fives. The plans for the widespread expansion of nursery schools is not intended simply as a child-minding scheme to enable mothers to go to work, but as a means of giving children half-day long opportunities for play under teacher supervision, with adequate facilities and in company with other children. There is also the considerable expansion of the playgroup movement where local mothers pool their resources and ideas and, in many cases, attend courses to give them greater insight and understanding into the nature of social play.

THE PLAY SPIRIT IN MATHEMATICS

In the traditional school, arithmetic was the most obvious example of the transition from play to work because it involved 'sums' which were always right or wrong. The rules for manipulating numbers were *given* by the teacher, not *discovered* by the child and much store was set on speed, either in mental arithmetic or in sum calculations. Of course, some children became efficient at the tasks set but for others there was a sense of bewilderment and failure, especially since so much credit was attached to accuracy.

The great changes which have come about are partly due to a fundamental rethinking by teachers of the nature of mathematical concepts; partly to a realisation, following the investigations of Piaget, that children acquire mathematical concepts slowly and only after a considerable period of practical work; and partly because mathematics is seen as a creative subject present in everyday life and in the environment and therefore as suitable for play activities.

With young children the appropriate play was chiefly concerned with discovering the meaning of 'more' and 'less' and 'equal' and with the various fields in which these relationships might be found, i.e. length, area, volume and weight. At a very early age children become acquainted in their play with numbers, and counting is a familiar form of play with infants. Sorting objects out into sets and matching them into a one-to-one correspondence are activities important for mathematical concepts and satisfying the criteria of play—imagination, freedom and social experience.

In 1964 the Nuffield Junior Mathematics Project was launched and gradually the old-fashioned arithmetic books, with their long series of exercises, were replaced by teachers' guides which were intended to help teachers design their own play activities for their own children. The aim was stated to be 'to devise a contemporary approach for children from 5 to 13'. The stress was on how to learn, not on what to teach and the central notion was that children must be free to make their own discoveries and think for themselves, and to achieve understanding instead of learning mysterious drills. The project began in fourteen pilot areas, but has spread since so that there are few schools that are not in some measure influenced by it. Many books have now been published along the new lines and a vast quantity of apparatus has been made available for practical work.

Teachers have felt the need for some over-all plan so that there is a degree of progression. The Nuffield *Teacher's Guides* suggested 'computation and structure', 'shape and size', and 'pictorial representation' as a possible scheme. The Essex County Council scheme, which may be taken as representing recent developments divides the mathematical course into three stages without prescribing age limits. Children complete each stage at their own pace though roughly the stages correspond to Piaget's three stages of intuitive thinking from 5 to 7 years, concrete operations from 7 to 9 years and logical thinking from 9 to 12 years. For each stage there are four main fields: sets; space; continuous quantities; and mechanical devices, such as see-saws and gears; and in each field children will be given experiences of physical properties, pattern and construction, measurement, counting and number systems, and operations. Practical examples are used such as the trundle wheel, rotating arm, thermometer, Meccano mechanisms, simple calculating machines etc. In the first stage, for instance, there are suggested activities such as arranging sets; building up a number line; making a simple abacus; collecting and sorting shapes; constructing with three-dimensional objects; playing with various forms of mosaic patterns; and comparing and recording personal measurements such as height, weight, hand span, foot size etc. It is stressed that although from the child's point of view all these activities take on a play character, from the teacher's point of view they represent fundamental mathematical ideas such as comparison, equivalence and grouping.

THE PLAY SPIRIT IN MUSIC, MOVEMENT AND DRAMA

If mathematics is the long-established subject in which the play spirit has only recently intruded, music, movement and drama are the comparative newcomers in which it has been strong from the beginning. Music has had a place in the primary school curriculum for many years but traditionally it has been associated with the singing of national and folk songs because, as the 1931 Report maintained, 'nothing could form a sounder foundation for a musical education'.[12] The ability to play the piano was once regarded as a highly desirable, if not essential, skill for the primary teacher. Since then many changes have come about. The percussion band has come into use as the means of cultivating rhythmic sense. The piano has disappeared from many homes in favour of the TV set and teachers are more likely to play the guitar than the piano. Recorder playing has become immensely popular and is probably now the main means by which children learn to sight-read music. In many schools there is now a room specially set aside for music where instruments of all kinds are available, from very humble home-made ones to those more sophisticated. Children are encouraged to form their own orchestra not only for school assembly but also for music-making. The range of singing activities has also increased enormously, partly under the influence of school broadcasting services. Indeed radio in the home has had a profound influence on the musical appreciation of primary children. On the debit side there is a dearth of competent music specialists and a consequent tendency for the responsibility for music to come into the hands of the comparatively few.

The idea is gradually gaining ground that music is so essential an element in the aesthetic and emotional education of young children that it should be incorporated more fully into the whole curriculum. One way in which this can be done is by introducing music into any and every part of the day—at assembly, at story-time, during social studies, and in language, or even mathematics, lessons. Another

[12] *The Primary School*, HMSO, 1931, p. 149.

approach is to integrate it more firmly with other expressive arts, notably movement and drama.

In so far as there is a case to be made out for teaching children national and folk songs there is an equally strong case for teaching them national and folk dancing and older children are quite capable of reaching a high standard in morris- and sword-dancing. Greek dancing and eurythmics can also be taught with much pleasure and profit. The influence of Laban has been immensely important in making movement an essential part of the primary school curriculum and this almost inevitably demands the introduction of music. Most modern teachers of movement use a record-player for their musical accompaniment, but this lacks the versatility of the skilled improvisator who can quickly stimulate class feeling. However, for most teachers this is not possible and therefore much attention must be given to the selection of appropriate records.

The distinction between music and physical education is also rapidly being discarded and music and movement are now inseparable. There is, nevertheless, still plenty of scope for the P.E. lesson in which a child is given freedom to test out his skills in physical movement in such play activities as ball throwing, jumping over obstacles, climbing, turning a cartwheel, etc. The typical P.E. apparatus of today in the primary school consists of various kinds of climbing frames, anything in fact which will help the child to explore his environment in terms of space, weight and time. In some schools the attempt is made to turn the playground into an adventure area by using a wide variety of objects against which the child can test his strength and skill with reasonable safety.

Music and movement naturally lead on to drama and here we remember that a great deal of children's natural play is of a dramatic nature. They project themselves into other characters, leaving those with which they are most familiar in the home background and identifying with those which are farthest outside the realm of everyday life, i.e. the giants, witches, heroes, and spacemen of their fantasies. Imitation is one of the commonest features of child play and its function is really one of enabling the child to extend his experience beyond the ordinary and to control, through identification with others, some of the ordinary experiences which he finds most intense.

Therefore the teacher is building on a sure foundation in using music, movement and drama for emotional expression. The function of music in this respect is obvious. Movement, which often approaches dance, is a natural means of emotional expression, whether of the joyful or tragic kind, whether showing aggression or fear. However, it is to spontaneous drama that we must look particularly for opportunities for imaginative play. This may occur at various levels and a few examples may illustrate the range. A teacher of young children telling a story may encourage her children by her own example to put into action the various movements involved: when the wind roars the children shrink back from it, when the child is lost in the forest they simulate her movements. Or the teacher may tell the children to pretend that their classroom is a ship and then they take on the various roles of captain, engineer, helmsman, passenger, man overboard and so on. Glove puppets are a favourite way with many teachers for getting infants to identify themselves with their characters; and drama arises naturally out of the project or the history lesson—for instance, the reception by the Red Indian tribe of messengers seeking the pipe of peace or Vikings saying goodbye to their home folk as they prepare to sail to Greenland. A more ambitious example, but one still within the capacity of juniors, is that of suggesting a theme, say the spreading of rumour, and inviting the children to build up a sequence from the quarrel between rival gangs, to the bystanders hurrying off to tell their neighbours, to the newspaper reporters questioning witnesses and finally to the production and circulation of the news.

If music, movement and drama are to keep the spirit of play it is clear that spontaneity and improvisation rather than audience performance must be emphasised. At the same time, children may often wish (as part of their play) to show others what they have done. It may well be that the public performance of written plays is beyond the capacity of most primary children, but there seems no reason why they should not from time to time give a 'concert' to another class or to a group of visitors specially invited. This is not so formal an occasion that they become self-conscious but, at the same time, the fact that others are interested gives them extra motivation and, one often finds, more verve.

FURTHER READING

Athey, A. J. and Rubadeau, D. O., *Educational Implications of Piaget's Theory* (Ginn, 1970).

Boyd, W. and Rawson, W., *The Story of the New Education* (Heinemann, 1965).

Boyce, E. R., *et. al.*, *Activity Methods for the Under Eights* (Evans, 1962).

Cass, Joan E., *The Significance of Children's Play* (Pergamon, 1970).

Chapman, L. R., *The Process of Learning Maths* (Pergamon, 1972).

Courtney, Richard, *Play, Drama & Thought* (Cassell, 1968).

Crowe, Brenda, *The Playgroup Movement* (Allen & Unwin, 1973).

Drew, C. E., *Modern Maths in the Primary School* (Ward Lock, 1970).

Entwistle, Harold, *Child-centred Education* (Methuen, 1970).

Evans, K. M., *Creative Singing—The Story of an Experiment in Music and Creativity* (OUP, 1971).

Fairclough, Gordon, *The Play is not the Thing—Drama in Education* (Blackwell, 1972).

Frith, J. R., *Playground Games and Skills* (Black, 1970).

Furth, H., *Piaget for Teachers* (Prentice Hall, 1970).

Garnett, Hugh, *Music Making with Juniors* (Schoolmaster Publishing Co., 1971).

Goodridge, Janet, *Drama in the Primary School* (Heinemann, 1970).

Hart, Joseph K., *Education in the Humane Community* (Harper, 1951).

Heritage, Raymond S., *Learning Mathematics* (Penguin, 1966).

Hodgson, J. and Richards, E., *Improvisation* (Methuen, 1966).

Isaacs, Nathan, *New Light on Children's Ideas on Number* (ESA, 1960).

Jordan, D., *Childhood and Movement* (Blackwell, 1960).

Joseph, Ann and Parfitt, Jessie, *Play Groups in an Area of Need* (NFER, 1972).

Lofthouse, Peter, *Dance* (Heinemann, 1970).

Lowndes, Betty, *Movement and Drama in the Primary School* (Batsford, 1970).

Mann, Beatrice F., *Learning through Creative Work* (National Froebel Foundation, 1971).

McLellan, Joyce, *The Question of Play* (Pergamon, 1970).

Midwinter, Eric, *Patterns of Community Education* (Ward Lock, 1973).

Miller, Susanna, *The Psychology of Play* (Pelican, 1970).

Morgan, Elizabeth, *Practical Guide to Drama in the Primary School* (Ward Lock, 1968).

Pape, Mary, *Growing up with Music in the Infants School* (OUP, 1970).

Pemberton-Billing, R. N. and Clegg, J. D., *Teaching Drama* (ULP, 1965).

Pickard, P. M., *The Activity of Children* (Longmans, 1965).

Ranger, Paul, *Experiment in Drama* (ULP, 1970).

Richmond, P. G., *An Introduction to Piaget* (Routledge & Kegan Paul, 1970).

Roberts, R., *Musical Instruments made to be Played* (Dryad, 1965).

Roberts, Vera, *Playing, Learning and Living* (Black, 1971).

Sealey, L. G. W., *Creative Use of Mathematics* (Blackwell, 1961).

Sellick, R. J. W., *Education and the Progressives, 1914–39* (Routledge & Kegan Paul, 1972).

Sturmey, C. (ed.), *Activity Methods for Children under Eight* (Evans, 1949).

Tansey, P. J. & Unwin, D., *Simulation and Gaming in Education* (Methuen, 1969).

Taylor, John & Welford, Rex, *Simulation in the Classroom* (Penguin, 1972).

Walters, Elsa Hopkins, *Activity and Experiment in the Infants School* (National Froebel Foundation, 1971).

Weber, Lillian, *The British Infants School and Informal Education* (Prentice Hall, 1971).

Chapter 7

Interest

Interest may be defined as a feeling of concern and caring. We are interested in what we believe to be relevant to our needs, what we think will bring satisfaction and pleasure, what will be to our advantage. Our interests matter to us, and we seek to pursue them whenever possible. Though to some extent we find an interest 'interesting' we may, on occasion, sacrifice one interest which seems attractive in favour of another which seems more satisfying in the long run.

Clearly, the 'interests' of teachers or parents and those of children will not always coincide, and then the question must be faced as to whose interest should have priority. Teachers of previous generations, and many of the present, would have no hesitation in deciding and their arguments in favour of ultimate teacher domination are quite strong.

They would point to the immaturity of children and their lack of experience concerning long-term effects. The child's-eye view is necessarily narrow and immediate. Such interests as they have are largely determined by their home and social background and cannot therefore be said to have been initiated by them. When interests clash children tend to choose what is more immediately interesting, which may not always be in their best interest; this is a problem in many homes about television-watching. The essence of a real interest is that it should be pursued in face of difficulties and frustration, but this is seldom the case with children; in their play they flit from one interest to another and, though this may be right in the context of play, it would lead to aimlessness if continued too long. Then there is the problem of defining the teacher's role. As the appointed representatives of society, teachers surely have a duty to promote the interests held by most people to be worthwhile. They have been selected and trained for this function and in the process have acquired a stock of knowledge and skill. While those who argue this way would reject any suggestion of dragooning and repressing unhappy pupils, they would assert that the initiation of those pupils into worthwhile interests was their clear duty. Essentially, their function would be to foster interests which look promising, to awaken those as yet unperceived and to curb those which are unprofitable. Clearly there is a dilemma when children covertly or, as today, overtly reject the interests which teachers urge upon them and this calls for tact and diplomacy. In a situation of potential rebellion persuasion is better than force but, in the last resort, force must be available. The extent to which persuasion—perhaps bluff is a more appropriate word—is used must depend upon the situation. What is possible with five-year-olds might be impossible with adolescents. What is feasible in a small village school might lead to chaos in a large city one.

Those who feel this way need not look far for philosophical justification for their opinions, as quotations from two doughty defenders of human freedom may demonstrate. Immanuel Kant says:

'One of the greatest problems of education is how to unite sub-mission to the necessary restraint with the child's capability of exercising his free-will—for restraint is necessary. How am I to develop the sense of freedom in spite of the restraint? I am to accustom my pupil to the restraint of his freedom and at the same time I am to guide him to use his freedom aright. Without this all education is mechanical and the child, when his education is over, will never be able to make use of his freedom.'[1]

The other quotation is from that stout opponent of any restraint upon the right of the individual to follow his own interest consistent with the rights of others, John Stuart Mill. Yet he abandons his own principle of the sovereignty of each individual 'over himself, over his own body and mind' in the case of children: 'It is perhaps hardly necessary to say that this doctrine is meant to apply only to human beings in the maturity of their faculties. We are not speaking of children, or of young persons below the age which the law may fix as that of manhood or womanhood.'[2] With children, in this respect, he couples 'those backward states of society in which the race itself may be considered in its nonage'.

Now for the arguments on the other side! First there are some negative arguments: the failure over many centuries of schools to satisfy a large proportion of their clients, the fact that however coaxingly a horse may be drawn to the water trough only he can drink the water in it, the tendency of teachers to regard their particular store of knowledge as a vested interest, the devotion of schools to highly questionable objectives represented by the examination system, the pursuit of goals which may benefit some children but are harmful to others. Positively speaking, there is the argument that the general history of education shows that the moments of growth in its content and method are also the moments

[1] Kant, Immanuel, *Über Pädagogik, c.* 29.
[2] Mill, John Stuart, *Essay on Liberty* (Collins, p. 135).

most in sympathy with some aspects of the pupil's freedom. Therefore whatever difficulties may be encountered in the search for freedom, they are worth risking. Then there is the argument that the affective element is crucial to the learning process. Unless a learner gets some pleasure from what he is doing the learning will be unsatisfactory. This does not mean that he will not be frustrated at times, but he will accept this willingly. Herbert Spencer put this point strongly, i.e. that the final test of all culture-value is whether it creates a pleasurable excitement in the pupils. Teachers tend to be suspicious of children's interests because of their superficiality and temporariness, but this suggests that their real task is to reinforce whatever interests are present and not to try to impose others for which the child is unready. There may be good social reasons for compulsory education, but there are few educational ones because unless there is some desire to learn what schools have to offer teachers become gaolers not teachers. The initiative for learning must come from the learner's existing interests, otherwise initiation is only into bondage. The new role of the teacher envisaged by this interpretation of his task is that education is a reciprocal process in which both parties learn together.

THE STUDY OF CHILDREN'S INTERESTS

Before considering the specific problems of studying children's interests we will make a few observations about child study generally, since this has become such a prominent feature in teacher training, especially for primary teachers. Child-centred enthusiasts looked for great help from the scientific study of child development. This hope may be illustrated by a quotation from a book which was popular some forty years ago, Nancy Catty's *Theory and Practice of Education*. Her opening sentence is as follows: 'For the purpose of child study it is useful to isolate the child from his environment, to regard him as a self-conditioning unit and to collect what knowledge we can obtain from psychology and kindred sciences as to the characteristics and endowments we can expect.'[3] Few psychologists today would attempt to 'isolate a child from his environment' but nevertheless there are dangers of isolation from reality in the scientific study of children as such. First, the method of studying behaviour and not self-consciousness has disadvantages. It may be reasonable enough in the case of animals and babies but becomes increasingly doubtful as self-consciousness develops. Second, the establishment of norms of development based on the study of large numbers of children under controlled conditions is open to criticism. Arnold Gesell, using these

[3] Catty, Nancy, *Theory and Practice of Education* (Methuen, 1934), p. 1.

methods, presents us with what he calls the 'profile' of the child of different ages. The problem for teachers is that they are dealing with individual children who deviate more or less from this hypothetical norm. The children we teach are individuals not deviants nor conglomerates of statistical data. Third, there is the danger that in formulating stages of development adjusted to chronological age the infinite variety and adaptability of human beings will be overlooked.

Complementary to the method of statistical normality is that of case study, in which individuals as such are studied in order to pinpoint all the factors operating. This also has weaknesses. It is inevitable that anyone seeking to do this scientifically must start with some theory rather than with open-minded observation. The tendency is then for the observer to make the child conform to the theory. A Freudian will 'discover' quite a different child from that which a Jungian will discover, and this is particularly true if any attempt is made to uncover the latent forces at work. It is difficult enough if investigation is confined to overt behaviour, but as soon as covert motivations are taken into account the subjective point of view of the observer inevitably intrudes. At a humbler and less clinical level of child studies, as carried out by students and teachers, there is a dilemma between the informal approach aiming at forming a relationship with the child and the scientific approach subjecting him to a battery of tests. Either way there are difficulties. The child is neither an intimate companion nor a detached specimen.

The study of children's interests must take account of the various meanings which may be attached to the word 'interest', and we suggest four:

1. *Interest as Hobby*   The essence of a hobby is that it is something done for the pleasure which it affords. It is pointless to ask someone why they are pursuing a hobby because the answer is obvious: 'I like doing it.' Let us take a typical family of three children—a girl of 11, a boy of 9, and a girl of 6. The elder girl is particularly interested at the moment in clothes. She looks through her mother's women's magazines and enjoys dressing up, and she was specially thrilled with her bridesmaid's frock for a recent wedding. She goes to a class in ballet dancing and is spoken well of by her teacher. She likes reading story books and writes quite imaginatively herself, for which she has achieved quite a reputation at school. She has recently acquired some pop records which she seems never to tire of playing on the record-player. She also looks forward to her favourite television programmes. The boy has quite different interests. He is extremely concerned about all living things and is quite determined

to be a vet when he grows up. He is fond of his dog, who is something of a trial to other members of the family. He loves to go for country walks with his father and to bird-watch, for which he has a good pair of binoculars. Though not aggressive, indeed he is gentle in his ways, he takes great pride in physical prowess and practises eagerly at running, jumping and playing games. He did join the Cubs but left because he found the programme boring. The little girl of 6 has very decided views of her own on most matters. She says she finds school 'boring' but is quite a competent reader. She shows great affection for certain dolls, in various states of disintegration, which she has kept since baby days. Her desire is to join in all the games and activities of her brother and sister, particularly of her brother. She has caught her sister's enthusiasm for pop records, and she professes eternal love for a boy slightly older than herself whom she will marry one day. These three children have a good store of toys and books which they share together very amicably and they are all willing to 'help mummy' whenever called upon so to do.

These children are unique only in the sense that all children are; and probably every child in every class would have his own special interests, with no two exactly alike. A teacher could, therefore, find out a list of hobby interests of this kind if he took the appropriate steps to do so. He could give his class a questionnaire asking them direct questions about television programmes, records, books, comics, toys, games, etc. No doubt in some cases the answers would be misleading but the teacher would get a fair idea of the hobby interests of his class. He could supplement this by asking them to write diaries, autobiographies, and journals or by requesting contributions to 'news times'. He could obtain further details from the parents or by observing children in the playground or after school.

2. *Interest as readiness to attend* Obviously a child's interests are not limited to his hobbies. There are many things that he is ready to give attention to because they have meaning for him, even though there has been no opportunity for him to develop a hobby from them. His readiness to attend will vary according to age, sex, social class, environment and personality. More than anything else, however, previous experience and expectation of experience to come will determine what is felt to be relevant, as, for instance, the death of a near relative or a mother's pregnancy. These are the factors that influence 'readiness' to learn more than the biological maturation presumed to be decisive by some progressivists. As R. F. Dearden says, 'The appearance of interests is being presented as the same sort of thing as the maturation of the nervous system . . . but this is a

disguised prescription.'[4] This is specially relevant to the learning of reading. The theory that reading readiness is dependent on chronological age is highly suspect; what is much more likely is that lack of motivation will delay reading almost indefinitely. About 17 per cent of school leavers are barely literate, unable to read at all fluently and incapable of writing. How is it possible that so many could have survived ten or more years of schooling without adequate remedial action being taken? The only answer possible is that after some experience of initial failure they mentally rejected reading and opted out of the educational system. Yet when they get out into the world and realise what a drag this deficiency is on their chances, and when they can be spotted and put in touch with remedial services they can and do learn without too much trouble.

To perceive a thing as having meaning is not just to understand it cognitively. There must also be *affective* meaning, and this is at least one meaning of interest. William James, in his *Talks to Teachers*, devotes two of his chapters to the problem of creating a new interest which, according to him, is essentially what teachers have to do. He says that the child has certain 'native interests' and that the art of teaching is to associate one of these with the artificial interest which is desired. He goes on to give an example of a 'native' interest: 'that which things borrow from their connection with our own personal welfare.'[5] Strictly speaking, a thing has meaning when acquaintance with, or knowledge about it, either enables one to infer or causes one by association to think of something else; but the original impulse is one of emotional involvement. This is what influences readiness to attend and the interests which flow from it.

3. *Interest as a 'felt' need* The 'felt' needs of the child may be equated with what William James calls 'native' interests and they may also be equated with that special class of needs which may be called 'wants', i.e. they are actively felt as desirable and necessary for happiness. Happiness is difficult to define because for each person it must have a different meaning, but in general it indicates reasonable contentment, some degree of hopefulness and capacity to recover from disappointment, and a certain balance between pleasurable tension and subsequent relaxation. In this there is an infinite range of possibility, from the bovine placidity of the mentally defective to the tortured triumph of the mountain climber. This is the inner condition to which there is an outer corollary in the adjustment of the individual to his physical and social environment.

[4] Dearden, R. F., *The Philosophy of Primary Education* (Routledge & Kegan Paul, 1968), p 30.

[5] James, William, *Talks to Teachers* (Longmans Green, 1913), p. 94.

Happiness depends on feeling tone, and this also takes numerous forms of which the following may be distinguished:

> Sensual pleasure in taste or colour.
> Free choice between acceptable alternatives.
> Admiration of an adored person.
> Sense of ownership.
> Responsibility for a dependant.
> Familiarity in family or group rituals.
> Surprise at the novel, unexpected or bizarre.
> Triumph, as in achieving an objective.
> Sympathy for a sufferer.

This is the sense in which those who believe in progressive education believe that interest is the motive of all work which, in the statement of policy of the American Progressive Education Association, 'should be satisfied and developed through . . . direct and indirect contact with the world and its activities.'

4. *Interest as a need of which the child is unaware* The problem about basing education on interest as need is that some felt needs of children are declared by adults to be unacceptable, e.g., the desire for revenge. Also there is often a conflict even in the child's mind between rival interests and someone has to decide on priority, and a great many things which adults may deem to be 'in the best interest' of the child make no immediate appeal to the child himself. Various attempts have been made to devise a 'hierarchy of needs' so that those of greatest importance can be emphasised. As an example, Herbert Spencer's *Essay on Education* may be mentioned in which he argues that the 'ultimate test' of all knowledge is 'its appreciable effect on human welfare' and concludes that 'it needs no long consideration' to discover that science is this most worthwhile knowledge. It is interesting to note, however, that a little further on he says that the 'final test by which to judge any plan of culture' is the 'degree of pleasurable excitement in the children'; and that 'even when, as considered theoretically, the proposed course seems the best, yet if it produces no interest, or less interest than some other course, we should relinquish it; for a child's intellectual instincts are more trustworthy than our reasonings.'[6] The *Plowden Report* gives five fundamental needs of children which education must seek to satisfy, but they are so general that they could be used as a slogan for almost any programme. The only way, it would seem, by which the unconscious needs of children can be put on an empirical basis

[6] Spencer, Herbert, *Essay on Education* (Everyman Edition, 1861), pp. 42 and 63.

rather than on an evaluative one is by taking a biological basis and by asking whether the notion of being human necessarily includes each of the following functions: Capacity

> To maintain a physical system.
> To detect a variety of stimuli from the environment.
> To operate on the environment.
> To relate to other people within a social framework.
> To acquire and organise knowledge and exercise control over volitional activities.
> To judge between alternatives and assign values.

Such a list may have some value as a framework within which to judge whether a total programme is justifiable, but it gives little guidance as to whether to teach a child French or not; indeed whether to teach him anything which does not fit in with his felt needs.

THE EXPRESSION OF INTERESTS IN SCHOOL

1. *Hobbies* There are numerous ways in which a school can make good use of its children's hobbies. Many schools have one afternoon per week in which children can bring their hobbies to school. This is an encouragement to those children who have well-developed hobbies and an incentive to those who have not developed any particular one. The teacher can guide individuals in developing a project arising from a hobby interest. Another fruitful suggestion is to form 'interest clubs' which can meet both in and out of school hours and exchange ideas, information and articles such as foreign stamps. Then again, hobbies may be made the basis for holiday projects so that when children return to school they may display work they have done or talk about their holiday activities. Short lectures on hobby interests are more likely to arouse attention from others if they arise from genuine experience. One function of the school might be considered to be the development of new hobby interests and, therefore, there might be alternative practical courses provided in which, for a term or more, children could learn book-binding or wood sculpture for instance. From time to time schools might have 'open-days' in which parents and others might be invited to see how hobbies could be developed.

It is essential for the success of schemes of this kind that the teacher should equip himself to share the hobby interests of his children. The 'alongside' position is a very good educational one since it makes possible a genuine relationship of mutual respect.

2. *Stimulating interests* In his day William James may have been right in saying that 'most schoolroom work, till it has become

habitual and automatic, is repulsive, and cannot be done without voluntarily jerking back the attention to it every now and then. This is inevitable, let the teacher do what he will'.[7] Conditions today may be regarded as far more conducive to voluntary interest and intrinsic motivation but, nevertheless, few teachers do not have some members of their class or some days in the week when attention flags and interest wanes. Part of the art of teaching is the devising of suitable methods for overcoming this lapse of attention. If he is speaking to the whole group the teacher must cultivate a lively manner. He must give every child the feeling that he has him in the corner of his eye. But encouragement and eternal vigilance will not always suffice and so the teacher must consider whether incentives can help. A good example of this approach may be seen in the Dalton Plan described by Helen Parkhurst in her book, *Education on the Dalton Plan*, published in 1922. Essentially, her scheme was that the pupil should develop an interest by being given responsibility for organising his own programme of work. She thus describes the system,

'Each pupil is classified as a member of a form, and for each form a maximum and minimum curriculum is drawn up. At its inception it lays the whole work proposition before the pupils in the shape of a contract job. The curriculum is divided up into jobs and the pupil accepts the task appointed for his class as a contract. The younger children are expected to sign a definite contract. As every month of the year has its own appointed task, a contract-job for any one form comprises a whole month's work. . . . A pupil must not be permitted to continue the study of any major subject beyond the limits of the month's assignment unless he has completed his contract in every subject. . . . Not more should be required than the pupils can easily accomplish by a wise division of their time.'[8]

Many teachers find it necessary to devise some scheme using stars, badges, credits or points which will accomplish the purpose stated for the Dalton Plan of giving 'work dignity and to the pupil the consciousness of a definite purpose'. And, what is more important, the hope is that by such means children will develop genuine interests in things which previously held no attraction for them.

3. *Expression of 'felt' needs* Interests are developed by being communicated and since language is the prime means of communication the teaching of the mother-tongue must emphasise interests. Since the formal teaching of grammar has largely disappeared from

[7] James, William, *op. cit.*, quoted by Knight, M., *William James* (Penguin, 1950), p. 238.
[8] Parkhurst, Helen, *The Dalton Plan* (G. Bell, 1922), pp. 28–32.

the primary school the real function of English as a subject is to provide various means, both spoken and written, of communicating interests to others. Some attention to standards is obviously necessary, i.e. the spoken word must be audible, the written legible; and the spelling must not be so far from dictionary correctness that comprehension is impossible, nor the sentence construction so unconventional that no one can understand it. But that is the criterion of correctness: that it must communicate. Formality is only a means to an end. Obviously the spoken word is the more natural but it is more difficult than in the case of the written to provide controlled situations for its development. The teacher must, therefore, spare no effort to encourage what has become known as 'oracy', and to devise ways in which as many children as possible can communicate with one another. This means developing the capacity to listen as well as to talk. The golden rule is that children should both talk and write on matters which genuinely interest them. The infant school tradition of 'news time' is something which might well be developed with older children. The problem is to give everyone a turn by having separate groups each with its own 'chairman'. Whatever experience individual children have had should be considered as a possible opportunity for either speaking or writing about it. The term 'creative writing' has come much into use recently but too often the only recipient has been the teacher. Ways should be devised, such as wall newspapers, class books, projects, and journals, which will encourage children to read each other's work. The one essential condition is that it must arise from a genuinely felt interest on the part of the writer. Increasingly the tape-recorder is being used in schools as a means of making language experience meaningful.

4. *Opening up new interests*　However child-centred education may become, the teacher always has a function in deliberately promoting interests which the child would never initiate for himself. Sometimes social conditions will help this stimulation, but not always. For instance, Dutch children find every encouragement to learn a foreign language because of their country's geographical and historical situation as a small nation depending on trade with larger neighbours who do not speak Dutch. In England this is not the case. Maybe the entry of Britain into the European community will eventually bring about a natural interest in a foreign language but at present it has to be deliberately introduced. Fifteen years ago French was being taught in a mere handful of primary schools but now this is a common thing. This change has been brought about deliberately by action on the part of teachers and authorities, and is an example of how new interests can be built up. It was in 1961 that the Nuffield Foundation

sponsored an experiment in which a French-speaking teacher showed what could be done with a small group of 10-year-olds by making French the only medium of instruction. Following this experiment there was an enthusiastic development of French teaching until, in 1963, the Department of Education set up a pilot scheme based on the teaching of children from the age of 8 by teachers who had been given special training in the problems involved. Consequently, in 1963 the Nuffield Foreign Language Teaching Materials Project was set up with the intention of producing suitable courses backed up by audio-visual aids. Tape-recordings were provided and a great variety of visual aids in order to avoid the use of English altogether during the French lesson. There is, of course, a problem in that if the group is large individual children do not get enough practice and therefore lose interest; so methods are being sought to make smaller groups autonomous, with the teacher playing an unobtrusive part in going from one group to another and only correcting where necessary. The intention of modern French teaching in the primary school is that it should be different from the traditional academic pattern and should develop a real interest in the French way of life.

FURTHER READING

Allen, Gwen, *et al.*, *Scientific Interests in the Primary School* (National Froebel Foundation, 1960).
Britton, James (ed.), *Talking and Writing* (Methuen, 1967).
Britton, James, *et. al.*, *Language, the Learner and the School* (Penguin, 1969).
Burstall, Clare, *French in the Primary School* (NFER, 1970).
Calder, Clarence R., *Techniques and Activities to Stimulate Verbal Learning* (Collier Macmillan, 1970).
Clegg, A. B., *The Excitement of Writing* (Chatto & Windus, 1964).
Cole, L. R., *Teaching French to Juniors* (ULP, 1964).
Cutforth, J. A. and Battersby, S. H., *Children and Books* (Blackwell, 1962).
Davie, Ronald, Butler N., Goldstein, H., *et. al.*, *From Birth to Seven* (Longman, 1972).
Dewey, John, *Interest and Effort in Education* (Houghton Mifflin, 1913).
Dixon, John, *Growth through English* (OUP, 1966).
Dearden, R. F., 'Instruction and Learning by Discovery', in R. S. Peters (ed.), *The Concept of Education* (Routledge & Kegan Paul, 1967).
Harding, D. H., *The New Pattern of Language Teaching* (Longman, 1967).
Holbrook, David, *English for the Rejected Child* (CUP, 1964).
Holmes, Neil, *The Golden Age for English Creative Work in the Primary School* (Macmillan, 1967).

Holt, John, *How Children Fail* (Pitman, 1964).

Komisar, B. Paul, '"Need" and the "Needs" Curriculum', in Smith & Ennis, *Language and Concepts of Education* (Rand McNally, 1967).

Marsh, Leonard, *Alongside the Child in the Primary School* (Black, 1970).

Molloy, J. S., *Teaching the Retarded Child to Talk* (ULP, 1966).

Schools Council, *French in the Primary School*, Working Paper No. 8 (HMSO, 1966).

Stern, Catherine and Gould, Toni, *Children Discover Reading* (Harrap, 1966).

White, A. R., *Attention* (Blackwell, 1964).

Wilkinson, A., *The Foundations of Language* (OUP, 1967).

Wilson, P. S., *Interest and Discipline in Education* (Routledge & Kegan Paul, 1971).

Yardley, Alice, *Exploration and Language* (Evans, 1970).

Chapter 8

Co-operation

THE CONCEPT OF CO-OPERATION

Inclusion of co-operation in a study of key concepts of primary education could be justified in several ways. The state of society internationally, nationally and at the individual level indicates a high degree of tension, aggression and disorder which bodes ill for the future of mankind. Technological advance, significant in every other direction, seems powerless in this situation. We look hopefully, therefore, to education as the means by which a new generation might be less inclined to compete and more ready to co-operate with each other. Unfortunately the present position in schools does not encourage much optimism in this respect. Educational opportunity is increasingly available to all classes but the results have not so far increased social cohesion. The majority of children who do not succeed in the educational race become embittered and reject the values for which education stands. Those who do succeed in rising from one class to another by climbing the ladder of opportunity are motivated by egoistic rather than fraternalistic considerations. This sad fact points to the necessity for re-appraisal of the concept of co-operation. In the development of progressive education there has been a tension between individuality and sociality. Child-centred education seems to imply that if each individual is given both opportunity and guidance to develop his unique personality to its highest potential the result is bound to be good socially. But social good is also a condition of individual good. The two are complementary not consecutive. Therefore community-centred education is just as important as child-centred. John Dewey, at least, seems to give the greater emphasis to the social side of the equation. In one instance he points to the inter-dependence between learning and social experience, saying, 'knowledge that is worthy of being called knowledge, training of the intellect that is sure to amount to anything, is obtained only by participating intimately in activities of social life'.[1] In another passage he speaks of the connection between what he calls 'social spirit' and all aspects of educational activity, especially moral education, as follows: 'The great danger which threatens

[1] Dewey, John, *Schools of To-morrow* (1915), p. 63.

school work is the absence of conditions which make possible a permeating social spirit; this is the great enemy of effective moral training.'[2] He sees co-operation between organised groups as being just as important as between individuals as the following words show: 'Every expansive era in the history of mankind has coincided with the operation of factors which have tended to eliminate distance between peoples and classes previously hemmed off from one another.'[3]

The significance of co-operation may also be illustrated in the fields of psychology and sociology. In psychology there has been a tendency to assume an egocentric basis for human development from which the child has to be weaned away to a reciprocal one. But, as Ian Suttie has argued, from the beginning in the womb and at the breast of the mother the child's experience is one of a reciprocal relationship in which tender emotion is dominant (Ian Suttie, *Origins of Love and Hate*). In sociology the evolution of society is interpreted as a movement from a communal to an associational society. Whereas in past ages social relationships were based upon kinship, tribal loyalty and feudal allegiance, the position today is that social bonds are entered into by an implied or specified contract in which each member seeks his own rational advantage. Thus we have what is called 'organisational man' whose co-operative activities are largely controlled by his status in the bureaucratic machine. It could therefore be argued with some force that the school should give precedence to co-operation rather than to competition in its organisation in order to redress the imbalance created by mass society and by egocentric individuals.

Co-operation occurs at many levels of emotional involvement. The co-operation practised by those who love and serve one another freely is at the deepest level. Then there is the co-operation of good neighbourliness in which concern for the other's welfare and sympathy for his misfortune predominates. Then comes the combined effort of those who share together a constructive activity. Any programme, whether it be of what to do in the immediate future or in the long term requires previous thought and discussion, and co-operation occurs when those concerned hammer out their aims and objectives freely together. This participation in planning is a vital element in the concept of co-operation. Finally, there is the co-operation of compliance and consent. When all members of a community cheerfully acknowledge the force of law and abide by it and readily fulfil whatever responsibilities are cast upon them we may speak of it as a co-operative community. Co-operation is

[2] Dewey, John, *Democracy and Education* (Free Press Edn, 1966), p. 358.
[3] *Ibid.*, p. 86.

possible between individuals but also possible between groups, and sometimes there is a clash of loyalties when a member of a group finds himself in violent opposition to a member of another group with whom he may have no personal quarrel.

SOCIALISATION

Every society depends for its smooth running on there being a sufficient number of people who share the same values, follow the same patterns of behaviour and fulfil the roles ascribed to them. Children are not born with these capabilities and would never develop them without adult guidance over a period of time. Socialisation is the process by which this is brought about, much of it informally in the family and through the context of adult ways of living, but also formally by educational institutions. This idea is comparatively new. Until about a century ago socialisation of the masses was only minimally directed towards anything more than making them law-abiding and efficient workers. Socialisation towards actual participation in the exercise of power was reserved for the children of the élite minority. Although adult roles are no longer determined by birth, the educational system is still thought of as a method of sorting out children according to the status of their later occupational potential. It does not have much success in socialising the majority of its pupils. The 1944 Education Act used as its yardstick for educational selection 'age, ability and aptitude', but at least it left open the question whether there should be separate schools for different types of children at the secondary level. The adoption of the comprehensive system may be claimed by its supporters as a mechanism for equality but, in fact, it is much more an extension of opportunity for children from working-class homes to climb higher. Thus although the abandonment of 11-plus selection has freed the primary school from some pressure it has not relieved it of its function as a sorting-out mechanism.

Socialisation in the primary school has certain inevitable limitations. It is not possible to believe that modern society in England has a consensus of values and behaviour. Different social groups have different norms and the culture pattern which most teachers believe to be the right one is not necessarily shared by the parents of their pupils. Furthermore, even the middle-class norms which teachers represent are in a state of flux, as witness, for instance, the present controversy among them about compulsory religious assembly and religious instruction.

At present, socialisation as carried out by schools seems to be a conservative and reflective function. Society is socially stratified and competitive; therefore schools are bound to reflect this. They follow but cannot initiate social change. However, according to D. F. Swift, this view is 'not only too pessimistic. It is also poor social analysis'. He goes on to enunciate the conditions under which education might have a chance to become a 'prime mover' in social change. These conditions are that 'it needs to be widespread throughout the population, persistent in influencing the individual and it must be linked with the occupational structure in a more than subordinate fashion'.[4] As an agent of social change the primary school is in a strategic position in that it is relatively free from the pressure of public examinations. On the other hand, its relation with the occupational structure is subordinate. In so far as education determines occupation the secondary school has greater opportunity for influencing the distribution of power in society. But since what is needed is not so much a redistribution of power as an acceleration of co-operation it is to the primary school that we must look for a lead in this matter.

Already most primary schools would claim that they were socialising their children in the direction of greater co-operation. This is the ethos proclaimed at school assembly, at parent-teacher meetings and on all public occasions. Children are urged to work and play for the advantage of their group, team, class or school. Voluntary service is emphasised, whether this involves doing classroom chores or acting as unpaid teachers' aides. The class-teacher system lends itself to a family atmosphere, and this is accentuated by the fact that most primary teachers are women and the men are *in loco patris*. With infants the relationship is often one of maternal care and grateful dependence, while with older children it is often a kind of feudal fealty. Nevertheless, this is a low order of co-operation which has little carry-over into later years. A more fundamental examination of school organisation is necessary if social change is to be an acceptable objective.

CO-OPERATIVE GROUPING IN THE PRIMARY SCHOOL

Whatever organisational changes may be made in the manner of grouping children in the primary school two factors must be recognised. The first is loosely known as 'atmosphere' and this is something which an experienced and sensitive person can feel as soon as he passes the threshold of a school. The personality and attitude of the head teacher is crucial here. In general, atmosphere is determined by the kind of respect which teachers have for the children in their care. This can come from realisation of their potentialities as human

[4] Swift, D. F., see 'Further Reading', p. 86.

beings, i.e. not simply in academic attainments; from genuine
pleasure in their freshness and spontaneity; and from appreciation
of even the smallest advance in their learning. The normal positive
response of young children is one of the hidden rewards of the
primary teacher and through this it is possible to get great satisfaction out of the stumbling efforts of the below average, the socially
deprived and the mentally handicapped. The second limiting factor
is the school architecture and equipment. A school which is too
small for its numbers has obvious handicaps in group organisation.
The traditional 'elementary' school with rigidly separated classrooms
arranged round a central hall makes the single class unit almost
inevitable. The old-type village school, even with partitions, is often
more flexible because the numbers have often declined. Increasingly,
however, new school building is adapted to a variety of group organisations. Two types may be mentioned to illustrate this. In one case
the school is arranged in four sections around a central hall, each
with three classrooms catering for the classes of the same age group;
and adjacent to them is a common area which the classes use in turn
for special purposes. In the second case the common area is much
bigger so that there is room for craft and practical activities. Each
'class' has its own 'base room', well carpeted and home-like but
without furniture so that children can sit on the floor and enjoy
privacy. The large common area makes possible great flexibility in
group arrangements varying in size, purpose and composition.

The majority of schools are not purpose-built open plan and
therefore most teachers have to consider how far they can go in
making the traditional classroom have the advantages of space. The
aim must be to break down, wherever possible, barriers to co-
operative and individual learning. Co-operative learning implies that
children normally sit in groups where they can help each other and
work together. Individual learning implies that there must be the
maximum of freedom of movement and that materials are easily
accessible when needed. Every inch of space must be purposefully
utilised, including space in the adjoining corridors. Interest tables
and interest corners must be accessible. The child must know where
all the resources of the classroom are located and be encouraged to
use his own initiative in using them. The essence of open planning is
that the child should know where to find the books, the pictures, the
work-cards, the materials he may need for whatever purpose.

To be successful an open-plan classroom must be reasonably tidy.
Thus furniture must be arranged so that movement is not hampered.
Things must be stored, each in its appropriate place, with something
of the orderliness practised by the average shopkeeper. Therefore
children must be taught the necessity for putting things back where

they belong and the teacher must have a continual campaign for tidiness. Otherwise the open-plan classroom can quickly become a junk room.

The traditional class-teacher system has its merits. It makes the timetable very flexible since only certain activities have to be time-scheduled, for example, for use of the hall. The children get a sense of security and belonging. With modern classes of thirty or less, the teacher can get to know individuals and give each one appropriate treatment. He gets the satisfaction of feeling that any progress made is due to him. For some purposes he can teach the group as a whole since they are homogeneous in age and possibly in social class and ability. On the other hand, teachers cannot be equicompetent in all branches of the curriculum and there are bound to be gaps. The class teacher tends to be narrow in his outlook, feeling that his responsibility is only to his own class, and the children's social experience is limited to a closed circle. The more homogeneity or affinity a class may have the less likely it is that they will learn to tolerate and work with those different from themselves.

Ideally, children should be trained to co-operate with as wide a spectrum of their fellows as possible, and this implies that they should belong to different groups. They should have the satisfaction of working with those whom they choose, with those whom they resemble in age or other respect, but also on occasion with those who differ from them. The average primary school has about 300 or so pupils, which should give ample scope for a wide range of social experience. Also if the emphasis is to be on co-operation rather than competition, children should not be encouraged to score off each other or to associate status with the group to which they may belong. They should be enabled to feel that the whole school is their community with all its variety of age, sex, background, ability and interest.

A type of grouping which has been found to have considerable advantages in the infant school is vertical, or family, grouping. In this system a child joins a class when he starts school and stays with it, and with the same class teacher, until he goes into the junior department. There is no reason why this arrangement should not go on for another year in the case of first schools. It is in fact the arrangement in the small village school and has considerable advantages to set against the narrowness of social experience. Older children can look after the younger ones and give them stimulus and the situation is more in line with the family life of former times.

Then there are interest groups of different kinds, of which the games team is the most familiar example. Here children different in every other way find they have something in common. Hobby clubs, music groups, swimming teams—even a backward readers unit—

can bring together boys and girls, younger and older, middle class and working class, and they can be organised in addition to the more stable class to which the child may be attached. There is a place for the continuous group but it should not be exclusive and should be supplemented by a number of more temporary or occasional groups.

The group to which each child should feel a sense of belonging is that of the school as a whole. How far this is possible will depend on a number of factors such as the 'charisma' of the head teacher, the size of the school and the support of the parents, but there are organisational techniques which can facilitate it. Something akin to a prefect system may help to get the natural leaders from among the children to feel responsibility for law and order. Something like a school council with elected members from each age group may help all the children to get the feeling of participation if the members report back from each meeting with the head. The ritual of morning assembly often sets the tone for the day, and the religious emphasis which is given to this in denominational schools helps the children to feel the unity between school, church and home. Apart, however, from its religious significance on which the views of teachers may well differ, the assembly of the whole school gives opportunity for the expression of group solidarity. In many schools responsibility for school assembly is put on each class in turn and this gives individual children the feeling that they are serving the school. Open days, concerts, Christmas festivities, sports meetings, bazaars to raise money for extra facilities, exhibitions and campaigns for deserving causes all help to arouse and maintain *esprit de corps*. The occasional calling together of the whole school by the head for purposes of congratulation, warning or even reproof can be used as an expression of 'we-feeling' if care is taken to avoid promoting feelings of alienation. The sense of belonging to a community is heightened, not lessened, if the school is not inward-looking but builds up links with other schools, with other organisations and with other neighbourhoods. If any way can be found by which the school renders public service its intrinsic value becomes apparent to its members.

CO-OPERATION AMONG TEACHERS

Any scheme for increasing co-operation among children will be enhanced if there is good co-operation among teachers. Even in schools where the traditional isolated class-teacher system is used there will be many opportunities for teachers to help each other, such as through advice in the staff-room, through the sharing of facilities and equipment, through sharing responsibility for special events. Nevertheless, unless positive arrangements are made it is easy for individual teachers to carry on with a minimum of common purpose or co-ordination of effort. To bring this about must, in normal circumstances, be the responsibility of the head. Only he is in a position to organise regular staff meetings with sufficient time at disposal to consider seriously aims and objectives. Staff meetings are necessary to consider specific problems of organisation involved in such events as an open day or sports meeting. But there is also need for more extensive meetings to discuss such fundamental problems as the objectives to be striven for, the strategies and tactics necessary to achieve them, the methods and techniques which should be employed and the assessment and evaluation of results. This is necessary at all times, but particularly so at times of re-organisation such as the opening of a new school building, the changing from a two-tier to a three-tier system or when some innovation in the curriculum is being planned. In his conduct of the meeting the head needs to combine the leadership which is his ascribed role with the impartiality of a clerk trying to interpret the 'sense of the meeting'. It is always better to spend time in gaining unity rather than to come to a decision by a majority vote which leaves a dissident minority.

There is always a problem in finding a compromise between hierarchical policy-making and co-operation between equals. The first seems more efficient but it has serious defects in making for unhealthy interpersonal relationships and petty jealousy, In a hierarchical situation individuals tend to defend what they regard as their interests and to look for alibis for failure, and teachers are well placed to resist any change affecting their own well-tried methods. One possible alternative is that schools should be organised on a collegiate rather than a hierarchical basis so that, for instance, there might be a rotation of office or a delegation of authority to standing committees. Another line of thought is that teachers should meet periodically away from their normal work setting with its pressures and vested interests. M. B. Miles suggests the following ways in which more genuine teacher co-operation can be obtained: team training in techniques for improving interpersonal relationships; role workshop where those in authority meet to discuss their problems; organisational diagnosis where a work group concentrate on specific problems such as sex education; and organisational experiment where a group of teachers carry out an experiment to determine the value of some innovation. His argument is that only groups working together can carry out policy changes, not individuals.[5]

[5] Miles M. B. quoted in Hooper, Richard, *The Curriculum* (Oliver & Boyd, 1971), p. 393.

One of the arguments in favour of the teachers' centres now being established is that they will provide teachers with a meeting place away from their school to discuss their curriculum problems and development. The usual in-service training course run by 'experts' does not provide the conditions for individuals to feel really involved in policy making, i.e. a common problem, a responsibility to do something about it and resources available for the purpose. The Schools Council publication *Curriculum Development: Teachers' Groups and Centres* says on this point, 'the essence of curriculum review and development is new thinking by teachers themselves, as well as their appraisal of the thinking of others. Teachers should have regular opportunities to meet together. They should look upon the initiation of thought, as well as the trial and assessment of new ideas and procedures, as an integral part of their professional service to society'. Gradually there is coming about a new concept of the teacher's professionality which puts his work into a wider context than the school in which he works and leads him to seek the collaboration of his colleagues elsewhere. This extended professionalism is likely to put teacher co-operation on a wider basis than heretofore.

This tendency may be illustrated by reference to the Schools Council projects. Here a curriculum-development project is decided upon and a writing programme about it is organised. The next step is to find a number of pilot schools to carry out the programme and to train the selected teachers in it. Meetings of the project team and the teachers are held, at which the teacher-pupil situations are simulated at the adult level and there is subsequent discussion. The practice of the Schools Council is to assign an evaluator to the project whose function it is to discover whether the project is in fact achieving what it sets out to do, and in this there must necessarily be collaboration with the teachers concerned. Once the project has got under way there is the problem of extending it to as many other schools as possible so that it may become nationally known and, it is hoped, accepted. Thus at every stage teachers are involved in trying out an innovation, testing it and modifying the procedures.

Perhaps the most widely spread development in teacher co-operation in recent times is that of team teaching. The first attempts were made at Lexington, Massachusetts in 1957 and since then it has become widely adopted both in America and in this country in various forms. Essentially, it is a method by which two or more teachers, working together, assume joint responsibility for all, or a substantial part, of the instruction of a group of children. The variations are dependent on whether the teams are hierarchical or associative. At one extreme there is a highly structured organisation with team leaders, senior teachers, regular teachers, teacher aides, student teachers and clerical assistants. At the other there is an informal group of equals meeting from time to time to co-ordinate their efforts but either having no appointed leader or taking it in turns to act as chairman of the group. Most teams fall somewhere between the two. The obvious advantage of team teaching is that there can be a pooling of skills and strengths. The less obvious advantage is that the team situation forces teachers to co-operate and to learn from each other. Normally, there is an arrangement by which the advantages of the class-teacher system are not lost and each teacher has his own 'personal' group and home base. Group organisation can be very flexible so that during the course of a week a teacher may meet individuals, or small groups, or his own class, or a large group of a hundred or more. Team teaching has considerable benefits for teacher training in that the student has experience of a variety of teaching styles and techniques and joins in the group discussions, but it has the defect of making student assessment difficult. Team teaching may well become the pattern in the new middle schools where a compromise is sought between the class-teacher system and the subject specialism of secondary schools. Increasingly, through B.Ed. courses, post-graduate training, Open University degrees and the expansion of in-service training primary teachers will be well placed to contribute specialist knowledge to a common pool.

CO-OPERATION AND THE SCHOOL CURRICULUM

If we accept the thesis that co-operation is a 'good' to be emphasised as much as possible does this imply that aggression is a 'bad' thing to be exorcised as far as possible? This poses the question: how much are aggression and violence rooted in human nature and therefore common to all and how much are they a reaction against unfavourable environment and therefore only a problem in the minority of those who are frustrated by circumstances? There is much evidence from the biological, ethnological and anthropological point of view that aggression is an innate and automatic response to any frustration.[6] The positive value of aggression is maintained by Alfred Adler—provided it is kept in check by the development of 'friendliness' (*gemeinschaftslichkeit*). According to Adler every human being has some defect or handicap for which he strives to compensate and this striving for perfection, despite limitation, is the key to human achievement. Acceptance of this view would entail an

[6] cf. Lorenz, Konrad, *On Aggression* (University Paperback, 1966), and Storr, Anthony. See 'Further Reading'.

acceptance that some degree of aggression is not only inevitable but desirable, even in the mildest tempered. In which case there are two educational problems, namely, training in social control for the majority of children and remedial treatment for the minority who are so alienated by their home background that they are likely to be the vandals and criminals of the future. We will examine these problems in aspects of the school curriculum where they are particularly relevant.

Political Education

Politics is the art and science of government. Its necessity arises from the fact that in any complex society living under a common rule there are different groups with rival interests. Its function is to maintain order consistent with the toleration of these opposing views and values. Its justification is that it permits men to be free even though at times they will selfishly equate their own interests with the good of the community as a whole. Inevitably there is compromise and an interplay between opposing and co-operating forces. One group must not force its will upon another beyond a certain point and the decisions of the few must, in the end, depend upon the consent of the many. Thus politics is the art of the possible in any particular situation. But always overriding this there must be some degree of consensus about the common good and the ideals to which all should, in a measure, subscribe.

It is important to recognise that these factors operate in the school community as in the wider society. Neither will attain the ideal, but there are certain safeguards against despotism in both. Those who govern must be ready to accept criticism and complaint from those who are governed. Decisions, whether of politicians or teachers, must be subject to revision in the light of discussion, at whatever level. Edmund Burke once said, 'I have never yet seen any plan which has not been mended by the observation of those who were much inferior in understanding to the person who took the lead in the business' and this illustrates the point that human judgements are fallible and can always be improved by discussion. On the other hand democratic government depends upon an acceptance by the governed of the rule of law. Any individual or group declaring themselves by their actions to be above the law are undermining the foundations of the rule of law. This also applies in the school situation.

No one would pretend that democracy is easy to achieve or sustain. It depends upon a population who have been brought up from infancy to democratic processes of open debate, shared responsibility, reasonable consultation and active participation. It depends also upon a population accustomed to taking an interest in public affairs and able to identify themselves with the common good.

Today, children are accustomed to the 'news' even though the 'news' is so often of disasters and disputes. In the primary school they are made aware of their national history even though too often this is mostly concerned with war and violence. It may be a pity that the heroes held up for their admiration are so often examples of human aggression, and perhaps there is something to be said for school redressing the balance and bringing before children the good side of community life and the heroes of peace who have healed society's wounds. Of course this is no argument for whitewashing human affairs, but since history is largely a story of conflict it could be treated as a storehouse of politics in action, i.e. the struggle between opposing forces to achieve some degree of harmony. For instance the long tale of the Civil War involving the many rival interests of king, gentry, merchants and commoners makes sense if it can be shown to have led up to religious toleration and relative freedom of opinion. The Swiss struggle for independence is another example where it may be said that good came out of evil in the remarkable political constitution of that country, where each canton has autonomy, each language group its identity and yet where there is strong national unity. The tension between regional and central control, as in India at the present time, is always a struggle for the best possible compromise. It is often said that primary children cannot understand history except at the narrative or social life level. But the essence of history is its political character and there seems no reason why children should not be introduced to it without the encumbrance of dates or reigns.

History is being made all the time, but the difference between current history and history past is that the issues involved are so controversial in the first and can be looked at more objectively in the second. However, such topics as race relations, strikes, communism and urban violence are bound to come up. Indeed, it is important that children should discuss them. The problem is that, although their discussion is bound to be uninformed, if the teacher proceeds to give them the 'facts' he is in danger of indoctrinating them with his own interpretation. However, it is no solution to ignore or suppress such issues. They are politically loaded but the teacher can take a neutral position while still emphasising that ultimately they can only be solved by agreement and co-operation.

Yet children will never be brought to understand how clashes of opinion can be resolved unless they participate in the process themselves. They must experience political action from the inside. The study of parliamentary procedure is bound to be without much meaning to them, so we must come closer home. Perhaps a visit to the local county hall and a talk from the mayor, or even from the chairman of the sewage committee, might bring to children's awareness something of the conflict between the ideal and the possible. But it is even more important that in the school community itself they should have experience of representative government, of delegation of authority, of the making and remaking of rules and of being kept informed of all matters affecting their welfare. Even so, it is inevitable that the majority of individual children will not participate actively in the running of the school, and therefore the need for small groups has a significance in political education because, however small the group is, it does involve questions of leadership, of compromise, of acceptance of responsibility. Kilpatrick makes the point, 'Practice in the intelligent pursuit of group purpose is the key to the future'[7] and it may be that here is the key also to political education.

Moral Education
There is a close relationship between politics and morality. Both are concerned with an ideal of what ought to be—politics with the general good and morality with personal good. Both are concerned with what it is possible to achieve under existing circumstances— politics with the harmonising of conflicting forces, and morality with each individual living 'according to his lights', although they may be rather dim. Both are closely connected with the idea of co-operation as against competition and with love as opposed to aggression. But, whereas few teachers would question the importance of moral education, many would express doubts whether political education is either desirable or feasible for young children. In fact, however, the two are different aspects of the same objective.

What is the origin of morality? Some would say that it is the family situation because that is where the individual first learns what it means to be accepted as a person, learns that he shares this personal quality with others, learns the idea of mutual service without obligation being incurred. Some would say that the ultimate grounds for moral obligation must be religious since we must assume a moral law behind the universe which can only be explained in terms of its creator. The categorical imperatives that we should only act in a way that we would wish to become universal, and that we should treat other beings as ends in themselves and not as means to our own ends, would seem to indicate a divine principle whether recognised or not. Those who hold this view no longer speak with the same confidence as their forebears and many would challenge the

[7] Kilpatrick, W. H., *Philosophy of Education* (Macmillan, 1951), p. 262.

necessity for a god. Nevertheless, it is difficult to find any fundamental reason for goodness other than intuition. Of course, those who believe in the autonomy of ethics would say that reason must be the ultimate ground for morality. The problem here is that reason can only deal with facts as they are seen to be and 'you cannot get an ought from an is'. S. E. Toulmin tries to get over this difficulty at the end of his book *Reason in Ethics*. He says, 'The statement "This practice would involve the least conflict of interests attainable under the circumstances" does not mean the same as "This would be the right practice" . . . but the first statement is a good reason for the second . . . and if anyone asks me *why* it is a good reason, I can only reply by asking in return, "What better kind of reason could you want".'[8] Why indeed, but it is no real answer.

What, then can we say with confidence about moral education? First that it is closely connected with the family experience and must therefore seek to prepare children to be parents in their turn. Thus moral education and education for family life are closely connected. This is particularly important when, as now, many children have not got the secure and loving background of a stable family. Parents may be divorced, separated or estranged and the children of such parents are greatly in need of affectional relationships with others. They need also to have brought to their minds the possibilities of happy life through stories, through studies of family patterns in other cultures or ages, and through learning the skills of home-making. Second, moral education is concerned with service to others and with group co-operation. From this it follows that every opportunity should be sought in school for acting sensitively, sympathetically, and in a neighbourly fashion to others. This concern for others should be expressed both in face-to-face relationships and in a feeling of unity with all the deprived or handicapped or unfortunate in the world. There is in human beings a universal desire for acceptance and approval by others and this provides the motivation for co-operation. Third, moral education must pay regard to the necessity for rational judgements. Fallible the judgements may be and often little more than rationalisations of desire, but, nevertheless, to be moral means that one can give good reasons for what one chooses to do.

Morality has an inner meaning and an outer. The inner meaning is concerned with the quality of the motivation, whether it is simply egoistic impulse or super-ego compulsion or intuition made precise by reason. The outer meaning is concerned with actual relations with others, i.e. with behaviour, attitude, and expression of feeling. Take, for instance, the matter of telling the truth. In many cases of young

[8] Toulmin, S. E., *Reason in Ethics* (CUP, 1964 Edn.), p. 224.

children telling lies the motive involves little more than romancing and contains no wish to deceive or gain an advantage. But as he develops the child comes to realise that telling the truth is essential to a condition of trust between individuals and this will become a part of the self-image of one who can be relied on. Thus, there is the outer and the inner aspect, though during the process of development the child may have many mixed motives and degrees of expectation from others.

Moral education presupposes that there will be moral failures from time to time turning perhaps into antisocial habits and the teacher must face up to this situation. He must accept the necessity to act as a moral authority and say quite distinctly this or that is wrong. The danger here is that of becoming authoritarian; this must be avoided by refraining from threats and intimidation, by giving reasons for the imperative that are as genuine and convincing as possible, and by letting the child answer back if it is done reasonably. Rational authority is not insecure because it looks forward to the child providing his own reasons. However there will always be offenders and then the teacher has the unpleasant but necessary task of devising sanctions. There have always been those who believe that punishment is an essential part of moral education and they give various reasons for this. The most common is that wrongdoing demands in justice some retribution. The other is that wrongdoing needs to be punished in order to deter others. In both cases the argument is that the infliction of pain or unpleasantness is justifiable if it results in greater good, either in the reform of the individual or the deterrence of others. It is difficult to prove either proposition, and often the wrongdoing is really only either a threat to the teacher's authority or a case of forgetfulness or misunderstanding, neither of which is morally evil. In any case, teachers today have little scope for inflicting pain on children. Corporal punishment is frowned on by authority; keeping-in is often impracticable; doing 'lines' is absurd; giving black marks may be effective in the short run but it is usually very short. So what is left? Disapproval? Bluff? Referral to the head? It is essential for the purpose of moral education that whatever sanction is proposed should produce some degree of shame (not guilt) in the mind of the offender. Therefore two suggestions may be put forward—one that any rule which is made should be easy to understand, reasonable to observe and consistently enforced; the other that antisocial behaviour, which is the real offence against morality, is best dealt with by isolating the offender from co-operation with others for a short time. The period of isolation must be short because the essence of moral education is group co-operation. As for acts due to carelessness or plain stupidity, probably the best way of dealing with them is by the 'natural consequence' punishment advocated by Rousseau, then in some way damage is put right and the lesson is learnt.

FURTHER READING

Beggs, D. W., *Team Teaching* (Indiana Univ., 1964).

Beyer, Evelyn, *Teaching Young Children* (Pitman, 1972).

Cook, Ann, *The Head Teacher's Role* (Macmillan, 1971).

Cook, Ann and Mack, Herbert, *The Teacher's Role* (Macmillan, 1971).

Cox, E., *Changing Aims in Religious Education* (Routledge & Kegan Paul, 1966).

Erikson, Erik H., *Children and Society* (Penguin, 1969).

Evans, K. M., *Sociometry and Education* (Routledge & Kegan Paul, 1962).

Forward, R. W., *Teaching Together* (Exeter Univ., 1971).

Freeman, John, *Team Teaching in Britain* (Ward Lock, 1965).

Hunter, Elizabeth, *Encounter in the Classroom* (Holt, Rinehart, 1972).

Klein, J., *Working with Groups* (Hutchinson, 1961).

Kohl, H. R., *The Open Classroom* (Methuen, 1970).

Lawton, Irene & Ridgeway, Lorna, *Family Grouping in the Infants School* (ULP 1968).

Lunn, Joan B., *Streaming in the Primary School* (Froebel Foundation, 1970).

Moore, Peter, *Co-operation Between Schools* (Exeter Univ., 1973).

NUT Report, Open Planning, 1974.

O'Neill, Margaret and Warrall, Michael, *Team Teaching in the Primary School* (Newcastle Univ., 1972).

Seaborne, Malcolm, *Primary School Design* (Routledge & Kegan Paul, 1971).

Stenhouse, Lawrence, *Discipline in Schools, Symposium* (Pergamon, 1967).

Storr, Anthony, *Human Aggression* (Penguin, 1971).

Swift, D. W., *The Sociology of Education* (Routledge & Kegan Paul, 1969).

Thelen, H. A., *Classroom Grouping for Teachability* (John Wiley, 1967).

Warwick, David, *Team Teaching* (ULP, 1971).

Wilson, John, *et. al.*, *Introduction to Moral Education* (Pelican, 1967).

Wilson, John, *Education in Religion and the Emotions* (Heinemann, 1971).

Chapter 9

Communication

MODES OF COMMUNICATION

The concept of communication is closely linked with that of co-operation. Indeed it is closely connected with the concept of education itself and with all the other concepts which flow from it. To receive a communication from the outside world is to have one's experience changed and therefore to have formed a new interest, however minimal. But to communicate an experience is to modify one's own attitude to the experience. Thus both the communicator and the recipient are in a way co-operating with each other. As Dewey says, 'Not only is social life identical with communication but all communication (and hence all genuine social life) is educative.'[1]

This is true even of communication where there is no personal exchange involved or where the personal element is far removed. It takes place in the form of signs, as when we interpret smoke as an indication of fire. Such signs may be made more accurate by human intervention as, for instance, by the provision of a thermometer which we read and use to obtain information to help us make decisions when cooking or to judge the weather. The intention of the communicator is a little closer in the case of road signs where we follow instructions about driving hazards, we might say that we are co-operating with the public of which we form part in order to avoid accidents. Part of the process of education is to teach children how to observe signs in the external world.

Mass communication plays an enormous part in modern life and here there is a combination of the personal and impersonal elements. Newspapers always try to tailor their news, gossip or entertainment to the point of view of the reader and they use every device to convince the individual that the message is for him or her. Radio and television rely on the voice, personal appearance and mannerism of the news reader or telecaster to establish a reciprocal feeling with the audience. President Roosevelt was one of the first and most successful exponents of the fireside manner which enables a man to speak to millions of homes as if he were a friend to each of them. But

[1] Dewey, John, *Democracy and Education* (Free Press Edn, 1968), p. 5.

mass media are bound to be impersonal, and the recipient is, for the most part, passive and non-participating even though recently the tendency has been towards drawing the public in by interviews, letters, invited audiences and telephone calls. The child of today is growing up in an environment in which he is daily, even hourly, bombarded by up to the minute happenings all over the world, by advertising of every conceivable material good and by highly processed entertainment. As Marshall McLuhan tells us, mass media have reconstituted dialogue on a global scale. In comparison the techniques of communication as used in the classroom must seem amateurish and old-fashioned.

Nevertheless, the most important mode of communication is that involved in face-to-face contact between individuals. Here also there are variations in the degree of personal contact and therefore of reciprocal feeling involved, but with children the emphasis is on the personal level. Whereas the mass media are bound to assume a consensus of background and experience which does not, in fact, exist, communication between persons who know each other is adjusted to particular circumstances and patterns of living. At the most intimate level there is communication between members of the same family where there is an element of affection but also shared assumptions and attitudes which are peculiar to that family. It is not simply by what is said that the communications of the family are effective. Each family has its own way of life; its own way of dealing with money, pleasure and trouble; its own method of settling disputes; its unique subcultural or ethnic assumptions, and this is the most permanent thing which is communicated to the growing child. As he gets older he will normally mix with other children who will further communicate to him their values and ways of behaving. In imitating others in his peer group the child will further reinforce or modify the attitudes which he has received from the family. So he comes to school with a built-in conception of the world and of his place in it.

Both the family and the peer group of the child will bias him towards a social-class outlook and it is now obvious that this will profoundly influence the way in which he will participate in the educational system. Traditionally, the public system of education is geared to the middle class both in the aims of the curriculum and in the selection of teachers. The popular explanation of the academic superiority of the middle-class child is that he has had the benefit of a more stimulating home environment and may have inherited higher intelligence. It is nearer to the truth to say that the working-class home communicates a different set of values and attitudes from those accepted in the education system.

Obviously the school has an important part to play in communicating to the young the cultural experience built up over many years, and in doing so it has developed three modes. The traditional one is that of the lecture or formal lesson, the essence of which is that knowledge is structured and systematised by the teacher so that the listener or reader takes cognizance of it. Communicating is then an intellectual exercise. The listener is stimulated, or at least kept awake, by questioning and subsequent discussion. The inadequacy of this mode is evident in many situations and in its place the methods of the workshop were introduced, in which teacher and pupil develop the same kind of relationship as that of master and apprentice; in other words the initiation model. The essence of this is a mutual participation between the two where communication takes place in concrete situations and as necessity arises. It is not by intellectual analysis, but by collaborative pursuit of a common aim, that knowledge is communicated. Even this approach, however, is not suitable for all situations. It is not suitable when dealing with the younger children, where a mode of communication has been developed which could be described as 'conversational' because the approach is as informal and unsystematised as possible, and where the teacher is prepared to take the more passive role and wait for the initiative of each child to show itself. Each of these modes has a place in primary education. There are points at which the intellectual presentation of a theme is appropriate, even as there are situations where the awakening of interest has to be waited for and the initiative has to lie with the learner. The best teachers are able to make their teaching genuinely child-centred.

LANGUAGE COMMUNICATION

It is the possession of language which, above all else, enables man to communicate and therefore some brief discussion of its characteristics must be made before we can consider its place in education. Language is defined by Simeon Potter as 'a system of arbitrary vocal symbols by means of which human beings communicate with each other'.[2] From this definition several points may be noted. One is that the basis of language is the vocal form from which writing is derived. Then, although the symbols of a language are quite arbitrary, they acquire through use an affective link with the things they represent. W. B. Yeats puts this in poetical style when he says, 'All sounds evoke indefinable and yet precise emotions . . . or, as I prefer to think, call down among us certain disembodied powers whose

[2] Potter, Simeon, *Modern Linguistics* (Deutsch, 1957), p. 36.

footsteps over our hearts we call emotions.'[3] And, though the primary function of language may be interpersonal, language has an important secondary function in making it possible for the individual to communicate with himself and thus provide the framework within which thinking takes place. Indeed the very way in which we think is largely determined by the linguistic framework which we employ. We could say that our minds are conditioned by our speech.

Generally it is the written language which is stressed in schools, despite frequent pronouncements from authority about the importance of the spoken word. Literacy is taken to mean the ability to read and write and even in the most progressive schools the staple activity is some form of writing, whether in projects, creative English, answering assignments or workbook tasks. Several reasons for this emphasis might be suggested. Written language is more syntactically organised than spoken language and may therefore be presumed to have more intellectual challenge in it. Though, as Bacon says, speaking makes a ready man, writing makes an exact man and reading a full one; and exactness and fulness are peculiarly appropriate for school objectives. Then it could be said that the written or printed word has great advantages over the spoken in that the eye is a better instrument for comprehending than the ear. In reading one can adjust one's speed to suit one's understanding and reading speeds can be increased very much more than listening speeds. The great advantage of reading over mass media is that one can choose what to read and when, whereas in radio and television the range of choice is limited. It must be admitted that there is much disappointment over the failure in literacy of so many children, and attention is now being focused not so much on the problem of teaching children *how* to read as on creating in them the *desire* to read.

The emphasis on written rather than spoken language is partly a practical one. Attainment in reading and writing can be more accurately assessed than speech. It is more relevant to the eventual taking of examinations. It is impossible to give individual children as much practice in speaking as in writing in a class of thirty or more, and in any case the children who need most practice are always the inarticulate and inhibited ones.

However, in terms of communication skills there are strong arguments for a greater emphasis on spoken language. Written language can only be built on a firm foundation of speech. This may be illustrated by reference to the teaching of immigrant children who come to school with very little knowledge of English. To try to get

[3] Quoted by Ogden, C. K. and Richards, I. A., *The Meaning of Meaning* (Routledge, 1923), p. 45.

them to read before they can talk with reasonable fluency is effort in vain. Oral skill must have priority in time and in emphasis. To some extent the same applies to children from culturally disadvantaged backgrounds. Bernstein's argument about the restricted language of the working-class child is that the latter is sadly limited when he comes to school 'in the type of stimuli to which he can respond'. He illustrates this point by contrasting responses to a mother saying to her child, 'I'd rather you made less noise, darling' and saying, 'Shut up'. Both may mean the same thing in the end but there is a big difference in the way in which the language structure in the first case mediates the relation between thought and feeling. 'Language' says Bernstein, 'exists in relation to a desire to communicate; consequently the mode of a language structure induces a particular form of the structuring of feeling.'[4] This is relevant to the argument about whether language teaching should emphasise the intellect or the sensibilities. Even in speech experience in school there is this division between those who favour the discussion/lecture model and those who give more importance to the imaginative, affective side of language through improvised drama, role playing and simulation games. We are perhaps fortunate in having a language without many inflexions and therefore without such a gulf between colloquial, spoken communication and 'correct', written communication. Another reason for giving more emphasis to the spoken than to the written word is that modern technology has put at our disposal instruments for diffusing it, such as radio, television and tape-recorders, which may be as revolutionary in the twentieth century as the printing press was in the fifteenth.

Emphasis on the spoken word is, however, a redressing of the balance and whether through books or through recorded speech it is important from the educator's point of view that children should be initiated into the various 'communities of discourse' with which, in growing up, they are faced. A 'community of discourse' may be defined as consisting of all those who share a common vocabulary and understanding of concepts in a particular field of knowledge. For instance, those who become involved in a particular interest such as bird-watching or fishing or football come to share the language appropriate to these interests. Just as, though not perhaps in the same degree, physicists enjoy a common frame of reference so do football fans, and it is this which turns them into a 'community of discourse'. In a medieval village it was conceivable that all the

---

[4] Bernstein, Basil, 'Social Class and Linguistic Development', in Halsey, Floud and Anderson, *Education, Economy and Society* (Free Press Edn, 1961), pp. 292–3.

inhabitants had the same range of knowledge of agriculture, crafts, religion and folklore. This is no longer possible, even for the most gifted and industrious man. The volume of knowledge is far beyond any individual's comprehension. One result is the alienation of the many 'communities of discourse' so that there is a gulf between the arts and science, religion and technology, art and logic. It is certainly not possible for children at primary level to become familiar with any of the main communities of discourse but it could be argued, as P. H. Hirst has done, that they should be 'introduced as far as possible into the interrelated aspects of each of the basic forms of knowledge, each of the several disciplines.'[5]

To foster social and intellectual development through communication is an overriding aim of education since personality itself depends on contact with other persons. Normally such contact is most easily achieved through speech, which is justification for abandoning the old tradition that children in school should not talk to each other; it is also a justification for the open-plan school provided that there is enough space for children to talk together without disturbing each other. Then the close connection between speech and thought is generally recognised as implying ample opportunity for all children to express their experiences to others. Language is not simply a desirable follow-up to experience, it is essential to it. Nor is language simply a vehicle for information, it is just as much a means of emotional expression. The intellect does not develop in isolation but comes from a basis of hope and fear, desire and aversion.

Communication in school is not a minority interest but a necessity for all. In every school there are relatively disadvantaged children who because of environment or experience, physical or emotional disability find it hard to communicate with others. Such children may become aggressive or withdrawn and their problems form one of the main challenges to teaching skill.

Language communication takes place at different levels. Traditionally the most acceptable level was communication between teacher and class and this is still important. It is most successful when the teacher is sensitive to the response of his pupils. This demands a constant adjustment of language style to the audience which involves appropriate vocabulary, audibility, delivery and feeling. The greatest professional handicap is teacher verbosity, the corrective to which is the art of questioning. Good questioning has something akin to good

[5] Hirst, P. H., 'Liberal Education and the Nature of Knowledge', in Archambault, R. D., (ed.), *Philosophical Analysis and Education* (Routledge & Kegan Paul), p. 132.

conducting. It is a means of challenging the quick and encouraging the slow, of checking the restless and awakening the withdrawn. It is the means by which the lecture is transformed into a dialogue and passivity becomes participation. To this end questions which demand a right answer should be alternated with those which, being open-ended, lead to discussion.

It is, however, generally accepted that a great deal of teacher-pupil communication must be at an individual level though at first sight this might seem time-consuming since many problems are common to the group as a whole. The justification lies in the fact of individual differences but it puts the onus on the teacher to treat each one as unique. His skill lies in putting to each child a slightly different form of the same question to help individual understanding and dealing with each child's question as revealing individual difficulty. It is an unattainable ideal to do this perfectly but the attempt has advantages over *en masse* teaching.

Communication between pupils themselves is as important as between teacher and pupil. Much of this goes on informally in small groups of two or more but provision must be made for individuals to communicate with larger groups as an introduction to discussion. Two criteria must be kept in balance: first, that discussion should be open-ended; second that it should be structured. Too much informality leads to irrelevance and confusion; too little stifles freedom. There must be some structuring otherwise there is interruption which may lead to chaos but it may easily inhibit the flow of argument. There must be an accepted starting-point, an order of procedure and a method of conclusion but it must not be assumed that the teacher is the only one capable of acting as chairman, leader or initiator. Nor must it be assumed that the class as a whole is the invariable unit. The teacher's function is to suggest suitable frameworks for discussion and to select suitable leaders. Thus, for instance, a child may speak briefly on something which he is interested in. Or a suitable object may be put into the middle of a group as a stimulus for exploration. An item of news or a quotation or even a single word may serve as a starting-point. Many devices used by broadcasting may be taken over or modified such as *Twenty Questions, Any Questions, Open Forum, It's Your Line, So You Think You Have a Problem* and so on. They give shape and form to what might otherwise be rambling confusion. Nevertheless the form must not limit the free association which is the characteristic of good conversation. The argument must be allowed to develop its own momentum.

Since speech is the basis of thought, oral communication must be the staple method of schools. However, this need not diminish the importance of reading and writing as means of communication. The two go together since in both there is one who gives information, ideas or experiences and one who receives them. The giver must have his audience, whether one or a million, constantly in mind; the receiver must freely choose to give his attention. Thus communication through reading assumes an open and accessible library so that each child can browse or skip or concentrate on what interests him while communication through writing assumes that someone else (and not necessarily the teacher) is going to be interested in what is said and is not prevented by illegibility, incomprehensible spelling or sentences so obscure that meaning is killed. Thus both reading and writing as means of communication depend upon as much variety and freedom of choice as possible.

COMMUNICATION AT PROFESSIONAL LEVEL

Teachers belong to a 'community of discourse'. Closely associated with them are other professional bodies who more or less share the same interests and concerns. Thus there are a number of groups having responsibility, official or voluntary, for the welfare of families. They have developed in the past in response to particular needs and from time to time their efforts have been co-ordinated, for instance, in the recent unifying of social and health workers. Within the educational service itself there are school welfare officers, school medical officers and all those connected with the care of handicapped children. Then there are groups of professional people who come into contact with the schools at various times, local authority advisers and inspectors, HMIs, college of education lecturers, librarians, museum curators, and many others whose connection with schools is more occasional. Nor must we forget the large number of voluntary and religious workers: the Brownie and Cub leaders, Sunday-school teachers, ministers of religion, marriage guidance counsellors and so on. The list is a long one but all are, in one way or another, sharing with teachers the care of children. And amongst teachers themselves there are the divisions between the various stages of education and the different types of school.

It is hardly surprising that between all these groups there are difficulties of communication, and, in consequence, a certain amount of duplication of effort and unconscious competition. The reasons are not hard to find, they are lack of time, differences of status, built-in lines of demarcation of responsibility, professional etiquette and so on. The following extract from a recent article may illustrate the lack of communication, 'The average teacher doesn't get much help from any of the special services: contact with the doctor is often fleeting or non-existent; remedial teachers often take children out of the class rather than help the teacher in the class; educational advisers may visit only infrequently and the psychiatrist and social worker not at all'.[6] To which, no doubt, the people criticised might say that they get precious little help from teachers. In addition, there is the separation between teachers and research workers in various fields, especially those concerned with educational innovation. Finally, there is the fact that communication amongst teachers, even in the same school, is often at a low degree at the level of day-to-day work.

What can be done to improve the lines of communication between groups whose work is so closely related? Certain situations may be suggested either in which there is urgency or where communication is not too difficult:

1. Most urban schools have one or more problem families where absenteeism is chronic, where the child's maladjustment is due to home tensions or where he is sent to school in no fit state to learn. It seems clear that in such cases the teacher, the school welfare officer, the health visitor, the social security officer and anyone else concerned should join forces or at least keep in touch with each other and provide something akin to a family service unit. The same kind of urgency applies to the educational priority areas and areas with a high concentration of non-English-speaking immigrants. The recommendations of the *Plowden Report* and of the *Seebohm Report* on the social services supplement each other in proposing a combined programme of action, and this implies continuous communication between the parties concerned. This may well be facilitated by the creation of the new regional government authorities able to cover a wide field.

2. Communication at the professional level is one of the objectives behind the proposals of the *James Report* on teacher training. In the first two-year cycle for the diploma of higher education it is envisaged that students of teaching should not be segregated but be linked with others intending to enter various branches of social service. This would give a common background for a variety of people working for child welfare, and facilitate later transfer from one branch to another. The present tendency of the Department of Education and Science to link colleges of education with polytechnics is another indication of the bringing together of professional workers. The proposals for in-service training move in the same direction since all teachers will be expected, at some point in their

[6] Jack Tizard, *London Educational Review*, June, 1973.

career, to be released from school and mix at teachers' centres or elsewhere for discussion with colleagues in various fields.

3. Several specific examples of fruitful communication may be mentioned as examples of what is possible. Though the pattern varies, a considerable number of authorities have appointed museum officers who are also trained teachers to maintain close liaison with schools by providing kits, giving demonstrations, acting as museum guides and generally advising teachers on the use of museum facilities. Much the same thing applies to many library authorities who appoint children's librarians to give advice to teachers and their pupils on the selection of books, and who send out, on request, boxes of books or illustrations relating to specific topics for project work. At another level may be mentioned the school architects' branch of the Department of Education which keeps closely in touch with the Schools Council so that teachers and architects may confer on the design and equipment of open-plan schools.

4. A very important field in which communication is essential is that of research and innovation. There is, for instance, the National Foundation for Educational Research whose function it is to initiate, co-ordinate and disseminate research findings. Then there are the HMIs whose function is becoming increasingly that of facilitating communication of ideas such as those of the new mathematics in which the late Edith Biggs played such an important part. Even more fundamental is the work of the Schools Council which seeks to act as an 'agent of change' and whose leaders have realised that without continuous communication beyond the pilot stage curriculum innovations will be temporary and superficial. The communication must be two-way with advice and material coming from the Council and comment and criticism being fed back from the schools.

5. It is both natural and inevitable that people working in an institution should become inward-looking unless they are stimulated to look outside, and possibly some organisational framework is necessary to bring this about. For instance, the bringing together of a number of schools on a single campus provides the environment in which they can communicate. Similar to this is the idea of the Cambridge Village Colleges where different educational and social activities can be carried on in the same buildings. Some years ago there was established at Peckham in London an institute which seemed to offer good prospects of worthwhile communication between educational, social and medical services, and in which both children and their parents might come together with professional people.

COMMUNICATION BETWEEN HOME AND SCHOOL

This is probably the most important field of all; it was firmly endorsed by the *Plowden Report* with the result that in many places parents are now entering into the life of the school, and teachers are making efforts to win them over to their methods. The minimum programme for parent-teacher co-operation recommended by the *Plowden Report* suggests welcome by the school, meetings with teachers, open days, reports and distribution of information. However, it must be admitted that parent-teacher relations are strongest where either little children or bright children in middle-class neighbourhoods are involved. It is likely to be an important feature in the development of nursery education which is proposed by the Government in *Education: A Framework for Expansion* (Dec. 1972) as follows, 'that within the next ten years nursery education should become available without charge, within the limits of the demand estimated by *Plowden*, to those children of three and four whose parents wish them to benefit by it' (Chapter 3. Section 17). Since the mothers of these children will have to bring to, and collect from, school their three- and four-year-olds there is bound to be plenty of opportunity for informal discussion with the teachers.

Communication between parents and teachers occurs at the local level, but it is also operating at national level through such organisations as the National Federation of Parent Teacher Associations, the Confederation for the Advancement of State Education and the Cambridge Advisory Centre for Education, all of them federated in the Home and School Council and sponsoring specific projects in the field of home and school relations. Again, however, this is largely concerned with young children or middle-class children.

With the majority of parents there are still psychological barriers to be overcome. The expertise of primary teachers is not so well recognised as that of other professional people or as that of their secondary colleagues. Three quarters of them are women and this gives to the primary school a somewhat feminine image which deters men from coming to it. Teachers, on the other hand, are nervous that parents may interfere and adopt a critical attitude and they are doubtful about a parent-teacher association which is chiefly motivated by social considerations. There has always been hesitation about allowing other adults into the classroom while teaching is going on and some reluctance to take on social roles other than the instructional ones.

Nevertheless, the school is well placed to take the initiative in building bridges between itself and the outside world since it is the only institution to which *all* children go, and there are strong arguments for saying that the time is right for a major public relations effort if school education, as we know it, is to retain the confidence of the mass of people. Although a parent's main concern may be with the progress in academic terms of the individual child, he or she may be drawn in on wider issues such as homework, choice of books, control of television viewing, toys and holiday projects. This last is of special significance at a time when, in many cases, both parents are at work and children have long school holidays with only the temptations of the big city to attract them. Parks and recreation centres are often ill-equipped to hold the interest of junior children and there are many days when weather conditions are not suitable for outdoor play. To make adequate provision for leisure is a real problem for many parents and they give up the task in despair. Far more could be done to help them both in advice and material provision. A number of teachers do already take part in play centres organised by the local authority and get paid for doing so, but this is a largely unexplored field.

The more parents can become actively involved in the work of schools the more likely they will be to listen to what teachers say about the general problem of education. For instance, a number of schools are glad to accept the services of mothers who come in from time to time to listen to children read aloud—something for which the teacher has not enough time. Then there are schools that are glad to let an adult go for a visit to a place of local interest with a small group in order to get over the legal difficulties of letting children leave school unaccompanied. The law is now more liberal in its interpretation of the rule 'What precautions would a reasonable parent take?'. Even without this help teachers can be more adventuresome than they have been provided they get the prior consent of parents for extra-mural activities. Modern conditions of teaching in which individuals or small groups work informally are much more suited to the entry of adults other than the teacher, and most primary teachers today are quite happy that parents or others should come in to tell groups or the whole class about their work or their experiences or their memories of childhood. This gives an opportunity to get fathers to come in to speak about their special interests, such as pigeons or cacti.

Perhaps the most important development of the future, made possible by mass media, will be a nationally devised programme of parent education looking forward to the time when the educational role of the mother is recognised in the early years of infancy, and to when the role of both mother and father in the later years is given the weight which it deserves.

COMMUNICATION AND MASS MEDIA

Television has become an accepted part of most homes for nearly thirty years. The novelty has worn off but it is still a more potent influence on the minds of children than the school blackboard. The average child of primary age spends a considerable time of each week in watching the TV screen and he is just as likely to be interested in adult programmes as in those specially designed for children. A great deal of what he sees is educative, if not intentionally educational, despite the frequent complaints that programmes are demoralising and pernicious in their effect. What make the normal programmes mildly educative are not the technological gadgets but the personalities of the broadcasters, and the skill of the producers in presenting programmes in a psychologically stimulating way. Thus, although the primary purpose of television may be news and entertainment, the teacher must acknowledge its significance as an instrument of education. He must, therefore, familiarise himself with the programmes which his children are likely to watch so that at least he has common ground with them.

However radio and TV are also used for more strictly educational purposes and here the teacher is more directly concerned. The BBC has been the sole provider of radio programmes for schools since the late 1920s, but television school broadcasting has been shared between the BBC and the ITA since the late 1950s. Throughout this development it has been a principle that broadcasting was supplementary to teaching and could never usurp the position of the teacher in the classroom. Nevertheless there has been a movement towards direct teaching rather than the 'enrichment' programmes which were at first thought of as the main type. Then it is the teacher who becomes supplementary in preparing his children to watch and in following-up with them the active response suggested by the broadcast. Another development which has tended to make the broadcast take the dominant part is the introduction, in a number of city authorities, of closed-circuit systems. The advantage of these developments is that programmes can be more closely geared to local conditions and fitted in more with school timetables. The tendency has been to move away from entertainment to direct teaching, covering all stages of a subject from the infant level up though ostensibly still depending on the co-operation of a classroom teacher.

One of the great difficulties about British school broadcasting as compared, for instance, with French has been that British schools do not have standardised timetables. Each school makes its own arrangements and may find it inconvenient to adapt itself to the timing of broadcast programmes. In fact this is not such a serious problem in the primary school as in the secondary but in the primary school another factor must be taken into account. The essence of progressive education is that work is individualised or group-controlled and that it does not have to conform to time schedules. But a broadcast is bound to cut across the informality and spontaneity of an integrated day. It can, of course, be justified in the same way that a talk from the teacher to the whole class can occasionally be necessary or desirable. In any case there is no need for every child to drop what he is doing to watch a programme which for him may be irrelevant.

It must be admitted that many good teachers are not altogether happy about television lessons. They are somewhat at a loss to know what is their role in the broadcast lesson. Are they, like the children, simply passive recipients of what is given by the expert? They find that not all children are held by the magic of the screen and some get almost nothing from it. They are nervous that teaching may come to be dominated by mechanical techniques instead of being a face-to-face relationship. On the other hand, there are great advantages. At least in closed-circuit television the teacher is watching some of his own colleagues at work, and this demonstration of teaching technique must stimulate him to consider critically his own methods. And since local authorities setting up a closed-circuit system normally employ teachers as the broadcasters the team which produces a programme must gain immeasurably in considering how best to put over their objectives, and may eventually discover what are the best techniques for particular subjects.

Teachers feel, rightly, that they ought to be closely involved in school broadcasting, and many of them can be through prior consultation and subsequent feed-back although, because of the nature of things, only a minority can participate directly. Even for them there is a problem in the question which must come up from time to time, 'Who is in the end responsible, the teacher team or the TV producer?'. Presumably the teacher knows what is necessary for the children but the producer may claim to know what makes a good programme. Both have professional skills but communication between them may be difficult because their presuppositions are different.

FURTHER READING

Bending, C. W., *Communication and the Schools* (Pergamon, 1970).

Bernbaum, G., *Social Change and the School* (Routledge & Kegan Paul, 1968).

Bernstein, Basil, *Class, Codes and Control* (Routledge & Kegan Paul, 1971).

Blyth, W. A. L., *English Primary Education* (Routledge & Kegan Paul, 1964).

Brown, Roger, *Words and Things* (Free Press Edn, 1968).

Craft, M., Raynor, J., and Cohn, L., *Linking Home and School* (Longmans, 1967).

Douglas, J. W. B., *The Home and the School* (MacGibbon & Kee, 1964).

Erikson, E. H., *Childhood and Society* (Imago Publishing Co., 1963).

Firth, Brian, *Mass Media in the Classroom* (Macmillan, 1966).

Gibson, Tony, *The Practice of E.T.V.* (Hutchinson, 1970).

Goodacre, E. J., *Teachers and their Pupils' Home Background* (Froebel Foundation, 1968).

Green, L., *Parents and Teachers—Partners or Rivals?* (Allen & Unwin, 1968).

Hodgkinson, H. C., *Education, Interaction and Social Change* (Prentice Hall, 1967).

Hubbard, D. D., *Parents, Participation and Persuasion in Primary Education* (Sheffield University, 1972).

Komisar, B. Paul and McClellan, James E., 'The Logic of Slogans', in Smith, B. O. and Ennis, R. H., *Language and Concepts in Education* (Rand McNally, 1967).

Lawton, D., *Language, Social Class and Education* (Routledge & Kegan Paul, 1968).

Maclean, R., *Television in Education* (Methuen, 1968).

McLuhan, Marshall, *Understanding Media* (Routledge & Kegan Paul, 1964).

Miller, Gordon W., *Educational Opportunity and the Home* (Longmans, 1971).

Murton, Alice, *From Home to School* (Macmillan, 1971).

Musgrove, F., *The Family, Education and Society* (Routledge & Kegan Paul, 1966).

Poster, C. D., *The School and the Community* (Macmillan, 1971).

Powell, L. S., *Communication and Learning* (Pitman, 1969).

Raynor, J. and Cohen, L., *Linking Home and School* (Longmans, 1967).

Rubinstein, D. and Stoneman, B., *Education for Democracy* (Penguin, 1970).

Schools Council, *The Educational Implications of Social and Economic Change* (HMSO, 1967).

Sharrock, A. N., *Home/School Relations* (Macmillan, 1970).

Wilkinson, A., *The Foundations of Language* (OUP, 1971).

Winstanley, Barbara, *Children and Museums* (Blackwell, 1967).

Year Book of Education, *Communication Media and the School* (Evans, 1960).

Young, Michael and McGeeney, Patrick, *Learning begins at Home* (Routledge & Kegan Paul, 1968).

Young, Michael, *Innovation and Research in Education* (Routledge & Kegan Paul, 1965).

Chapter 10

Integration

INTEGRATION AND THE PRIMARY CURRICULUM

If by integration we mean the attempt to combine parts into a whole then there has never been a time when this was not the declared intention of curriculum constructors. For many centuries the education of those who were to be the leaders of society consisted of the acquisition of Latin. The methods employed for young children were deplorable, since what was required was the memorising of grammatical rules before they were allowed even to tackle the simplest Latin sentence. But the aim was admirable: to give them entry to the sources of European civilisation. R. S. Peters puts the case for 'classics' as the staple of the curriculum as follows:

'Surely the strongest case for classics is that it is a field combining many forms of understanding and appreciation. At a time when all sorts of rather artificial attempts are being made to contrive an integrated curriculum in which due attention is paid to "the whole man", classics stands as a well-established field of study which satisfies most of the criteria laid down by such educational theorists.'[1]

Much the same claim could be made for the elementary school curriculum as it developed in the nineteenth century. No doubt the treatment was mechanical and unenlightened, but the declared aim was to give to the children of the poor proficiency in the arts of learning, i.e. the three Rs, with some ideological understanding of the fourth R—religious education. Maybe it was not intended to have cultural value since it was predominantly and unmistakably utilitarian but it certainly gained some integration by its 'social utility'.[2]

When, at the turn of the century, attempts were made to broaden the scope of secondary education controversy settled on the problem of unifying the curriculum and there were two opposing points of view. That of Robert Morant—that secondary education must

---

[1] Quoted by Stenhouse, Lawrence, 'The Humanities Curriculum Project', in Hooper, Richard, *The Curriculum* (Oliver & Boyd, 1971), p. 337.
[2] Mannheim, K., and Stewart, W. A. C., *An Introduction to the Sociology of Education* (Routledge & Kegan Paul, 1962), p. 21.

preserve the values of the old humanistic disciplines—was successful and this profoundly influenced the primary curriculum. The defeated view was that of Michael Sadler who argued the case for a curriculum which would 'draw the subject matter of instruction very largely from those spheres of knowledge which are nearest to the pupil's present experience and to his probable career'.[3] Though today the attempt is still being made to broaden secondary education through the comprehensive system the repercussions of Morant's victory on the primary school are still evident, and there is still a tendency to equate the curriculum with a list of 'subjects'.

Nevertheless there have been constant attempts to integrate the 'subject' curriculum in one way or another. For instance, in a book on methods of teaching which was popular sixty years ago the author speaks of a fashionable doctrine, known as 'Concentration of Studies', in which a special topic was chosen as the 'core' of instruction around which all other subjects should be grouped, and says that a favourite 'core' in those days was *Robinson Crusoe*. Children were taught to read the book, to write exercises upon it, sing songs about Crusoe's life, draw the objects mentioned, work sums in terms of Crusoe's productions and so on. It is interesting that Mr Welton, the author, describes the scheme as 'fantastic' because it assumes that 'human life can be built up by the artificial arrangement of ideas' whereas the 'real unity of every life is a unity of purpose'.[4] This was roughly the argument put forward by the *Norwood Report* of 1941, which was as follows:

'We think it difficult to find any principle of what is called integrating the curriculum if it is to take place round a subject or a group of subjects, still less round a single idea such as, for instance, leisure or self-expression or citizenship. If anything is to be integrated it is not the curriculum but the personality of the child . . . only the teacher can make a unity of the child's education by promoting the unity of his personality in terms of purpose'.[5]

Of course this Report was concerned with the secondary stage, but there is an intimate connection between the secondary and primary stages and the Primary School Report of 1931 makes the point that 'it can hardly be denied that the primary curriculum is distorted and the teaching warped by the supposed need of a later educational

[3] Quoted by Graves, John, *Policy and Progress in Secondary Education* (Thomas Nelson, 1943), p. 43.

[4] Welton, James, *Principles and Methods of Teaching* (Univ. Tutorial Press, 1909), pp. 42–4.

[5] *Norwood Report* (HMSO, 1941), p. 61.

stage'.[6] The primary curriculum has always been dominated by the views of subject specialists who, according to Robert Dottrens, the author of a survey of primary curricula throughout the world, 'are the main cause of the over-loading of the curriculum and of the maltreatment of pupils whom the teacher tries to force to assimilate knowledge which has no cultural value, very often no practical value, and of which those who do not teach it are usually ignorant'.[7]

Integration of the primary curriculum is, therefore, dependent upon what is done in the secondary school, especially for the average and below average pupils for whom, according to the *Newsom Report*, the 'traditional subject divisions of the curriculum are artificial and restricting'.[8] The *Plowden Report* is somewhat more cautious in condemning secondary subject divisions though it does say, 'We stress that children's learning does not fit into subject categories. The younger the children the more undifferentiated their curriculum will be. Even for older children subjects merge and overlap.'[9] Voices have been raised recently against the ideology of the *Newsom Report* with its suggestion of a 'soft' curriculum for the majority of children and a more demanding one for the minority. One writer speaks of it as depressing and uniformly anti-intellectual' and urges that techniques should be worked out 'to help the less able to learn the *same things* as the more able learn more readily'.[10] In effect this is a plea for the kind of common education for all children up to the age of 14 which is claimed in the Soviet Union. From the age of 7 all children follow the same unified course with the above and below average advancing at the same pace but repeating any year's work in which they do not reach a satisfactory standard. But however successful such a system might be in Russia, it would certainly not commend itself to the majority of teachers in Britain who look for a different kind of integration than the formal one of a highly centralised course of subject studies. Nevertheless, integration of the curriculum is meaningless unless one's mind is clear about what is being integrated and the principles upon which it should be done.

INTEGRATION BASED ON THE CONCEPT OF 'WHOLENESS'

John Henry Newman says, 'I lay it down that all knowledge forms one whole, because the subject matter is one, for the universe in its

[6] *The Primary School* (HMSO, 1931), para. 74.

[7] Dottrens, Robert, *The Primary School Curriculum* (UNESCO, 1962), p. 123.

[8] *Newsom Report* (HMSO, 1963), para. 353.

[9] *Plowden Report* (HMSO, 1967), para. 555.

[10] White, John, 'Instruction in Obedience' in *New Society*, 2nd May, 1968, p. 639.

length and breadth is so intimately knit together that we cannot separate off one portion from another except by a mental abstraction.'[11] This is a fair statement of the idealist position, but what does it mean? We can only give tentative answers to such a profound question but each of them throws some light on possible ways in which education might be integrated.

1. The world as we see it is a mental picture making sense as a whole. Doubtless there is a physical reality behind it but what we perceive is a product of our own imagination. It follows that the sort of integration to be aimed at is in the mind of the pupil. Does he have a world picture that makes sense as a whole?

2. Although we constantly abstract portions of reality from the whole, the 'objects' so perceived cannot be isolated from their background without losing their character. Therefore every 'object' owes its significance partly to its own characteristics but partly to the web of relationships of which it forms part. It is impossible to put a limit to these relationships and, in that sense, the universe is contained in a grain of sand. Each separate 'object' is a microcosm of the macrocosm. Therefore integration means starting with something familiar and discovering as many as possible of the relationships which it implies.

3. Since each person has his own mental picture of the world, i.e. his apperception mass in Herbartian terms, it follows that any new experience is fitted into it. Therefore the process of integration is one of gradually expanding the picture by incorporating new experiences, and the task of the teacher is to select experiences most likely to accomplish this. Integration means enlarging an existing system of thought—pushing out bridges from it to adjacent islands.

4. To say that all knowledge forms one whole does not mean that each person's whole is the same; far from it. Nor does it mean that the whole is never distorted; it frequently is. We presume that the teacher has greater breadth of outlook and a more coherent picture of the world than the pupil and therefore that he can guide the pupil to discover new relationships. In this sense the *Norwood Report* is right in saying that it is the mind of the pupil which has to be integrated but this is a process which requires as much freedom on his part as possible to diverge from the obvious.

5. The wholeness of knowledge depends upon extending the range of what is relevant. Nothing is entirely irrelevant because, as Newman says, 'the universe is intimately knit together', but the discovery of this does not just 'happen' except to the mind prepared for it by an existing interest. The 'flash' of recognition of relevance comes to the

[11] Newman, J. H., *Idea of a University* (1852), p. 11.

mind ready to receive it. The teacher's function is to provide the stimulus most likely to lead to individual integration. What is an adequate system of thought will depend on the practical purpose of investigation. For instance, the system of thought in which the Sun is perceived as a bright disc up in the sky is not a false one if the practical purpose is to enjoy its heat. An astronomer's system of thought would perceive it as a mass of energy millions of miles away and the centre of the planetary system. An astronaut's system of thought would provide still another picture because he looks at it from a point of view other than the terrestrial one. In these days, projects on space have been made popular by lunar exploration and the child of today has a mental picture of the universe beyond the imagination of medieval man. At the same time it is doubtful whether children can really integrate the new cosmology into their picture of the universe simply by being shown models of the planets following their orbits round a symbolic sun suspended from the classroom ceiling. Integration of new ideas into old takes time to become genuine.

6. Each individual's system of thought, which for him is the wholeness of knowledge, is in some respects inadequate, distorted or ill-adapted for practical purposes. It does not form a satisfactory *Gestalt* or pattern. It lacks symmetry and the connections are insecure. In particular areas meaning is obscure. The facts involved are not clearly related to one another, so the system of thought has the character of a motley assortment. Integration may then be defined as the process of producing a more meaningful arrangement in which a consistent theme is developed, relevance to practical utility is demonstrated and the ideas involved make sense.

7. The wholeness of knowledge may be looked at from another point of view: that of development in time. Here we are concerned with the problem of causation, and two lines of thought are possible. One is to try to establish a chain of events in which each is the natural result of the preceding one and leads on to the next. This is linear development. For instance, a project on the history of transport might trace the line of development from coracle to Concorde. Each step forward solves one problem but raises another. The other line of thought is to discover how a number of factors come together to produce a certain result. For instance, a war comes about through a convergence, at a particular time, of a variety of factors—economic, social, religious, personal—which come to a head through some accidental occurrence. A diagnosis of disease is based on the assumption that if all the relevant factors could be discovered a rational explanation would be possible of why a particular person contracted, shall we say, cholera. We would first have to look at the symptoms

to make sure it was cholera. Then to the environmental factors which might have contributed, i.e. personal and public hygiene, possible contact with disease carriers, individual state of health and so on. Whether we are trying to establish a sequence of cause and effect for a war, an illness or an accident there is always a problem in deciding how far to go back in time and how many factors to take into account. The wholeness of knowledge indicates that the possible scope of an inquiry is infinite but we should take into account as many aspects as possible.

8. Many people believe that a rational explanation of human development must include reference to a divine being, from whom proceeds a universal law. Those who profess to follow the teaching of Froebel are apt to forget how central this was to his philosophy. Thus he begins his book, on *The Education of Man*, with this state-ment, 'In all things there lives and reigns an eternal law'. From this 'law' Froebel derived the rest of his theory of education—the 'gifts', the play spirit, the creative urge in children, the influence of nature—and he concludes his book with this account of educative occupations:

'They simply have the purpose to secure in the young human being all-sided development and the unfolding of his nature; they furnish in a general way the food so necessary for mental growth; they are the ether in which his spirit breathes . . . inasmuch as the mental tendencies which God has given him, and which irresistibly unfold from his mind in all directions, will necessarily appear in great variety, and must be met and fostered in a corresponding variety of ways.'[12]

These implications of the principle of wholeness open up a number of useful guidelines for the integration of the curriculum. New knowledge must always be incorporated into the existing frame-work, not stuck on. The existing framework must be strengthened by developing relationships with what is beyond it. Fruitful inquiry can start from any point in which interest is aroused but the resulting pattern of thought (the *Gestalt*) must be given strength (*Prägnanz*) by being arranged in a meaningful way. Integration presupposes an understanding of sequence in time, so that every event is seen as a link in a chain of cause and effect but also as a focus of an indefinite number of factors bearing upon it. Finally, integration is greatly helped if it arises from an ideology, either religious or political or philosophical.

[12] Froebel, F., *The Education of Man* (Tr. W. N. Hailmann, Appleton) pp. 1 and 327.

On the other hand, as a basis for curriculum construction, integration has certain limitations. The assumption that a child at any age is capable of following out a line of inquiry, with the teacher simply exercising a passive role of waiting to be appealed to, ignores the amount of guidance which is necessary for discovery to take place. We cannot overlook the fact that children's discovery is dependent upon both positive guidance and a given framework. Thus, there is always a danger that the integrated day so popular in the infant school as a protest against timetable rigidity will result in a formless day because there are no guidelines. The problem may be illustrated by the failure of the Nuffield Junior Science project begun in 1964 but which failed to establish itself in schools. The organizer, Ron Wastnedge, attributed this to a number of factors such as lack of time for preparation and of follow-up in-service support for teachers. His conclusion is that 'Nuffield Junior Science was essentially like all other national ventures. It created an enormous initial splash and the ripples became progressively weaker and modified with time and distance'.[13] It is possible, however, that the real cause of failure was that too much was expected from the spontaneous questions of children on any topic which happened to catch their attention. Hilda Taba in an article on the 'Conceptual Framework for Curriculum Design' criticizes the weakness of methods of curriculum development which 'omit the organizing of teaching units' and which thereby 'usually result in guides on paper which do not function in classrooms', and goes on to speak of the 'poor articulation between the levels of schooling, the perennial complaints by each level of lack of preparation on the preceding level, misplaced expectations, and a lowered amount of growth'.[14] Another writer on curriculum integration, Richard Pring, makes a similar criticism of a theory of the wholeness of knowledge when he says, 'Unity, integration, wholeness seem to have a fascination and value of their own. But what do they mean? "Integration" as such is an empty word. There must be integration of something and one cannot really understand or appreciate what it is that is being integrated until one has clarified what it is that is being integrated.' He goes on to argue that the wholeness of knowledge only makes sense when it is unified by some principle or within some framework. Thus he says, 'No enquiry can take place except within a particular system of thought . . . in a way it does not make sense to talk of

[13] Wastnedge, Ron, 'Whatever happened to Nuffield Junior Science?', article written for the Open University Course, E. 283, Unit 13.
[14] Taba, Hilda, *Curriculum Development: Theory and Practice* (Harcourt Brace, 1962), quoted by Hooper, Richard, *The Curriculum* (Oliver & Boyd, pp. 141–2.

children simply making an enquiry. It must be an enquiry of a certain sort.'[15]

It would seem therefore that what is needed is a framework within which a progressive sequence of learning activities can be devised, and a principle by which selection of this or that activity can be made. The framework and the principle must be broad enough so that nothing is excluded on grounds of irrelevance and yet firm enough so that nothing is included which cannot be integrated into the whole.

The school library is a good example of a framework within which learning can be integrated. To be successful it must be treated as a most important part of the school's resources with ample space, free access and a generous allocation of funds. The aim should be that any child or group should be able to follow up a line of inquiry in a number of directions, i.e. cutting across subject barriers. For this purpose the arrangement and classification of books must be understood by all and the children must be trained in the techniques of extracting ideas and information. The school library should be kept up to date and supplemented by magazines and visual material, and it might well include booklets and studies made by succeeding generations of children. Its function is to contribute to every aspect of the curriculum but also to provide an integrating structure for all.

However we must accept the fact that for many primary children the school library is not possible as a basis for integrated study. There are the children of the infant or first school still on the threshold of reading skills and the many older children who do not find it easy to browse or search in a library. Therefore we must look a little more closely at the principles involved in the infant school form of organisation known as the 'integrated day'. It may be that with modifications it is also suitable for older children with library work as just one of the activities offered.

Essentially the integrated day form of organisation is one providing a controlled environment which will be thought of by the child as a whole and in which he can choose what to do and how long to spend doing it. His activities are self-directed but within a framework which gives him a sense of security. The teacher's function is to maintain the degree of control necessary if things are not to get out of hand, to deal with individual children by encouragement and praise and to offer suggestions for activities which the children would not think of if left to themselves. Her problem is to see that progress in learning is made, and therefore she will normally have a basic daily programme which will include reading and writing arising from a self-

[15] Pring, Richard, 'Curriculum Integration', in Hooper, Richard, *op. cit.*, pp. 266–7.

chosen interest, experience involving mathematical concepts and some activities of a practical or creative nature.

It would be idle to pretend that simply to provide children with a variety of occupations from which they can choose and to abolish teacher-directed tasks will automatically give young children a sense of the wholeness of knowledge. But unless there is some awareness of this the integrated day easily becomes disintegrated, however busily the children may seem to be occupied. It is not sufficient that the child should freely choose to do this or that. He should choose because one thing leads to another. His reading, his measuring, his shopping, his painting, and all the other practical activities must somehow make his experience more coherent, more integrated in truth as well as in teacher's theory. No doubt this is not easy to attain. Children used to teacher-direction, children who are disturbed or maladjusted, children who have never had much chance for initiative may need a great deal of training before they can exercise the freedom implied by an integrated day organisation. Partial integration which is successful is the best preparation for complete integration later on. The fundamental criterion is whether individual children begin to form a coherent pattern of thought embracing all their varied experiences.

INTEGRATION ARISING FROM NEEDS

The assertion that education should aim to satisfy the needs of children is common in progressivist literature and it is well supported by official pronouncements. Indeed it has become something of a slogan which is interpreted as meaning that the child should be the centre of attention in all educational policy. As such it has some value because it does at least force teachers and administrators to feel that they must justify their policies by reference to the welfare and happiness of children. Indeed one writer maintains that the vagueness and multipicity of meaning of the term 'need' 'far from impairing its usefulness, enhances it. For its utterance in a slogan in a suitable setting may further or maintain some educational enterprise'.[16] But however useful the concept of 'need' may be in making education more 'child-centred' it has too many possible meanings for it to be used as a basis for curriculum design.

Nevertheless the concept does have a use as a framework within which children's inquiry may be guided. This is the way in which it is taken by John Merritt in a model for essential studies which he has

[16] Komisar, B. Paul, '"Need" and the Needs-curriculum', in Smith and Ennis, *Language and Concepts in Education* (Rand McNally, 1967), p. 41.

devised.[17] It is not intended as a model to be accepted or not but rather to show how an idea (namely 'need') can be systematically developed. It is at least a possible starting point.

Merritt begins with an analysis of the biological systems which together constitute our notion of a *human being*. They are as follows:

1. The physiological systems which enable a man to function and survive.
2. Those which enable him to perceive and respond to his environment.
3. Those which enable him to manipulate and operate upon his environment.
4. Those by which he relates to and co-operates with other human beings.
5. Those which enable him to acquire, organise and express knowledge.
6. Those which enable him to choose and make judgements and decide questions of value and priority.

Although each of the needs satisfied by one or other of the systems has a biological basis the study of them must be extended to cover all the tools, instruments, artefacts and institutions devised by man to facilitate their functioning. Thus bodily mechanisms have been enormously extended by mechanical inventions and social institutions. This opens up an unlimited field of inquiry in the physical and social sciences and their practical applications.

Furthermore, each of the biological systems operates upon something in the physical and social environment which constitutes its 'environmental correlate'. For instance, the digestive system depends upon the supply of suitable food; and the neurological system by which we think depends upon an appropriate language system. In each case there are considerable differences in the knowledge and understanding of individuals regarding what is necessary for efficient functioning, and part of the aim of education is to remedy any information deficit.

Then again, the six systems suggested are interdependent and inquiry into any one of them can be expanded into the other five. For instance, John Merritt shows how a study of diet as a means of satisfying the physical maintenance of life can be extended in other directions, thus:

1. The study of diet entails consideration of food necessary for human health.

[17] Merritt, John, 'A Framework for Curriculum Design', Unit 10 of Open University Course, E. 283, *The Curriculum*.

2. This involves knowledge of how we can recognise, classify and test such foods.

3. We go on to consider how such foods may be obtained from the physical environment.

4. This in turn demands study of the ways in which men co-operate to make food available where it is needed, i.e. agricultural economics, transport and marketing etc.

5. From this arise the unsolved problems where our knowledge about food production is inadequate.

6. Finally we might consider questions concerning food where value judgements are involved, for example, foods in which there is danger of addiction or of over-consumption.

What is at stake in such a concept of curriculum design is to find the best way of studying the nature of man, i.e. his innate resources, his motivations and modes of expression. This is the over-arching principle which could be interpreted in numerous ways of which the analysis of biological needs-systems is only one. Thus, for instance, the Keele Integrated Studies Project Junior Units, which could be used in primary schools, took three themes as 'core' topics— Exploration Man, Communicating Man and Social Man. The advantage of the needs analysis is that it is all-inclusive and arises from a basis of reality, whereas there is no logical reason why the three themes chosen by the Keele Project should be accepted rather than any others that might be suggested. It supplies a framework which gives due weight to the notion of the wholeness of knowledge and at the same time provides for a planning sequence which would make possible a common, but not a uniform, education.

The problem of integration in such a scheme may be looked at first from the child's point of view and then from the teacher's. Let us consider the child of primary school age. He is, in Piaget's terms, at the stage of concrete operations, that is, he is not yet ready to make abstract analyses of the nature of man or of his needs. In many cases, such as children from culturally deprived homes, there is an inability to pose questions worth investigating. The child's curiosity is restricted to the needs of the moment rather than to the needs of man in general. He may also lack the skills necessary for independent inquiry, reading for instance. Even if the child can read he may lack the ability to select and assemble material from books and may resort to copying out unrelated passages. In any case there are some children who find it more congenial to express their ideas in concrete forms rather than through words, i.e. in the arts. Nevertheless, with all these reservations the integration of knowledge must take the form of inquiry suggested by Dewey, that is to say, first the awareness of a problem to be solved, then the search for the relevant data, then the restructuring of the problem in the light of new knowledge so that a hypothesis is tentatively formulated, and finally trying out the solution in some tangible way. But many children will need help in this process.

For the teacher there are other problems. In adopting anything like a needs-based curriculum the teacher is undertaking an innovation for which his previous training has not equipped him and in which he is not supported by existing traditions. He is forced to organise his work in categories with which he is unfamiliar. Then the teacher must have regard to the particular limitations of the children he is responsible for. Some of them may need to be put into small 'nurture' groups where they can be given the experiences which more fortunate children get in their own homes. It is no use trying to push them into forms of inquiry for which they are incapable. It is extremely difficult to draw the line between guidance and direction, for while it is unrealistic to expect children to think out problems without stimulation or to investigate them without the appropriate resources it is mistaken kindness to give too much help. In the last analysis truth cannot be pre-packaged by one person for another. Each individual has to find his own way and the danger of elaborate 'packs' or 'kits' is that the learner is too much a recipient and too little an initiator. The correct balance between guidance and direction for the individual child may well be beyond the capacity of an individual teacher; it may call for team teaching so that one teacher can help a child in linguistic expression while another can deal with concrete or emotional expression. We must accept the situation that school education is necessarily artificial but it should be properly artificial, i.e. selecting, organising and accelerating the processes of real life. From this, it follows that the teacher's function is not just to wait patiently until questions arise spontaneously from the pupil any more than it is to push the pupil into investigations in which he sees no point. The teacher must have a goal and a plan for implementing that goal but he must be constantly revising and evaluating it in response to the reactions of individual pupils. From this point of view integration is the bringing together of the teacher's plan and the pupil's development of it. It does seem that there is some risk that packaged resource material such as that developed by the Goldsmiths College Curriculum Laboratory or by the Keele Integrated Studies Project will be treated too rigidly and with insufficient regard for individual differences both of schools and of pupils.

One obvious way in which integration can be secured with due regard for differences of schools and of individuals is in the study of the neighbourhood. As a means of natural integration this has unique advantages. Any neighbourhood can be looked at through the eyes of the subject specialists: the geographer looks at physical features and economic activities; the historian looks at buildings and arte-facts; the naturalist at flora and fauna; the scientist at technology and natural phenomena. But the different points of view are all united because the neighbourhood is a living whole. Furthermore, it goes beyond the subject boundaries because a neighbourhood is alive, men and women are working there, they are living in families, and their lives are conditioned by their environment. A local com-munity is an expression of culture according to the classic anthropo-logical definition of the 'complex whole which includes knowledge, belief, art, morals, laws, customs and other capabilities acquired by man as a member of society' (E. B. Tylor, *Primitive Culture*, John Murray, 1871, p.1.). Yet every community is different from any other and provides almost unlimited scope for individual approach and at any level of sophistication. Another great advantage is that local study opens up possible ways by which children can serve the community of which they are part and ways in which people in the community can serve the interests of its children. Thus it offers the possibility of integration between school and community through mutual service.

However, local study is most likely to be fruitful if it is carried out within a framework, so that one child or one class supplements the work of another. Indeed, the possibilities for co-operation are so great that many schools have made neighbourhood study a project for the whole group of teachers and pupils, and have mounted an exhibition for the interest and profit of parents and the public generally. This is where a scheme such as John Merritt's analysis of human needs can be profitably used because it covers every possible aspect of inquiry looked at from the standpoint of human beings:

1. The internal maintenance systems suggest topics such as food, clothing, shelter and health.

2. The respondent systems suggest topics such as temperature, humidity, sound, vision, colour and all the artificial devices employed in connection with them.

3. The operant systems suggest such topics as movement, exercise, physical labour, locomotion and, again, all the devices associated with them.

4. The co-operant systems suggest topics such as the family, local government, division of labour, clubs and societies and all the ways by which men and women practise division of labour and the sharing of responsibility.

5. Then local study might be concerned with all the ways in which

people in a neighbourhood communicate, receive and p
knowledge and experience through mass media and cultural ac

6. Finally there might be a study of all the ways in v
community expresses its beliefs and values through religious, c
and recreational institutions.

INTEGRATION ARISING FROM DISCIPLINES OF KNOWLEDGE

Many teachers would resist the idea of a 'needs-based' curriculum,
or any variation of it, as an alternative to a 'subject-based' curriculum
in which an area of knowledge is chosen because it gives good opportunity for inter-disciplinary integration. This indeed is the principle
behind the Keele Integrated Studies Project, and it is noticeable that
this concept of inter-disciplinary integration is mainly emphasised in
the field of the humanities. The same tendency does not arise in the
case of mathematics which is recognised as autonomous. With
science at the primary level the case for autonomy is not so strong
though it would be generally accepted. But in the subjects relating
to man the boundaries are felt to be artificial and unnecessary for
young children, however valid they may be for advanced study.
There is no need for them to be treated separately and the case for
integration is strong. It may call for a pooling of resources, especially
where some teachers may be deficient in practical skills and expressive
arts.

In grammar schools and institutions of higher education humanities
subjects are treated separately and this separation is not just one of
convention because they have behind them long traditions and well-
established disciplines. But if in addition, it is true that they represent
distinct 'forms of knowledge' or autonomous modes of understanding
then the argument would be that they should be kept separate even
for young children and the sooner the better. This does not rule out
inter-disciplinary integration but it does imply that the boundaries
must be kept clear. Each 'subject' would have its unique contribution
to make to the whole; each represents a distinctive point of view.
This is the argument of people who believe that differentiation is just
as important as integration. Here is the opinion of one such writer,
John White:

'In one sense of the term, an integrated curriculum is highly
desirable. But what I would like is a curriculum unified by a
rational principle. The separate disciplines should be seen as fitting
people to be members of the good society. This does not entail,
though it does not rule out, any fusion of the disciplines. But
"integration" in the Schools Council's sense has nothing to do with

any such rational principle. It seems in many cases to mean the virtual disappearance of the disciplines, their swallowing up in topic-based courses.'[18]

Official policy is ambiguous on this question, constantly emphasising that subject divisions are arbitrary and yet constantly employing them. For instance, the advisory *Handbook of Suggestions to Teachers* of 1942 says 'education should be thought of as a unity and not in terms of individual subjects ... which are no more than aspects of a many sided training', but it goes on to say 'it is convenient to deal with them one by one' and 'the curriculum may be likened to a fan, each leaf of which has its origin in the activities of the youngest children' (p. 157). Even the *Plowden Report* goes through the same procedure. Above all, the colleges of education insist on all students, primary as well as secondary, devoting a large part of their time to the study of a 'main' subject. The assumption is that because certain subjects have been developed at university level they must have some inherent value for anyone. R. S. Peters puts the argument in these terms:

'As a person seriously asks the question "Why do this rather than that?" he can only answer it by trying this and that and by thinking about what he is doing in various ways which are inseparable from the doing of it. When he stands back and reflects about what it is that he is doing he then engages in the sorts of activities of which the curriculum of a university is largely constructed. He will find himself embarking upon those forms of inquiry such as science, history, literature and philosophy which are concerned with the description, explanation, and assessment of different forms of human activity.'[19]

This may seem rather a weak argument for using these same subjects as the basis of the primary curriculum, even if they are brought together in broad topics. Paul Hirst, however, makes a more serious claim that there are a certain number of 'modes of experience and knowledge that are fundamentally different in character'.[20] This is quite consistent with the idea of 'fields of knowledge' in which several of the autonomous disciplines may be integrated, but each of these fields then must have its own standards of validity and its

---

[18] White, John, 'The Curriculum Mongers', in Richard Hooper, *op. cit.*, p. 279.

[19] Peters, R. S., *Ethics and Education* (Allen & Unwin, 1966), p. 162.

[20] Hirst, P. H. and Peters, R. S., *The Logic of Education* (Routledge & Kegan Paul, 1970), p. 63.

unique concepts since 'only where there is public agreement about the classification and categorisation of experience and thought can we hope for any objectivity within them'. Objectivity is the goal to which inquiry at any level should aspire and for this 'merely shared concepts are insufficient'.[21]

If we ask what it is which makes these forms of knowledge autonomous Paul Hirst provides us with four criteria:

1. They each 'involve certain concepts that are peculiar in character to the form.'
2. Each form 'has a distinct logical structure.'
3. 'Each form has distinctive expressions that are testable against experience in accordance with particular criteria that are peculiar to the form.'
4. 'The forms have developed particular techniques and skills for exploring experience and testing their distinctive expressions.'

He goes on to admit that 'the dividing lines that can be drawn between different disciplines by means of the four suggested marks are neither clear enough nor sufficient for demarcating the whole world of modern knowledge'.[22]

Nevertheless he does attempt to differentiate the forms of knowledge, though the lists which he puts forward differ from one place to another and he admits that some are a matter of long-standing dispute. Also he admits that 'the radical independence which each mode has is only one aspect of the situation. What is also important is the pattern of interrelationships between them'.[23] It will be readily conceded that over the years certain disciplines have evolved a distinctive character and that, as far as possible, children at the primary level should be initiated into these 'ways of knowing'. What is not so easy to accept is that there are a definite number of 'forms' which are inherently independent. For instance, there is little agreement amongst writers as to what these supposed 'forms' might be. R. F. Dearden lists six—mathematics, science, history, the arts, ethics and religion—and recognises that *all* our knowledge does not belong to one or other of these. He does claim, however, that they are 'basic ways in which human experience has, as a matter of fact, been extended and elaborated in the course of history' and must therefore be 'of great relevance to formal education, of which it is in

---

[21] *Ibid.*, p. 62.
[22] Hirst, P. H., 'Liberal Education and the Nature of Knowledge', in Archambault, R. D., *Philosophical Analysis and Education* (Routledge & Kegan Paul, 1965), pp. 128–30.
[23] Hirst, P. H., *The Logic of Education*, pp. 64–5.

:d of transmission'.[24] Another writer, Denis Lawton,
ive 'core' subjects: mathematics, science, the humanities,
;ive arts and morality;[25] while the *Newsom Report* divides
into three 'broad fields of experience': practical subjects,
the humanities, and mathematics and science.[26]

In view of such divergence of treatment it would seem that at
least at primary level integration is more important than differentiation, especially in the broad field of the humanities where the
distinctions are less obvious and in the expressive arts where overlap
between the arts and crafts and between different art forms is
inevitable and desirable. This leaves us with only mathematics and
physical science as distinct forms which must to some extent be kept
separate. For most purposes the curriculum must be planned according to sequences of topics in which thinking is unitary rather than to
disciplines to be mastered. As for the means of bringing this about,
various suggestions have been put forward. The most radical is that
there should be major changes in the pattern of training for primary
teachers with inter-disciplinary studies taking the place of main
subjects, and that this should be followed up by in-service training
along the same lines. But whatever is done to increase the range of
primary-teacher skills there will always be differences of interest and
expertise. This implies team teaching in which, although there may
be differences of organisation depending upon such factors as size
of school and age range of pupils, there is a much greater degree of
collaboration than has hitherto been common. Thus integration of the
curriculum depends upon integration of the teachers and this can be
facilitated in ways such as the following:

1. The accumulation of 'good' teaching practice by allowing
teachers to observe each other's methods and discuss their evaluation.

2. The harnessing of technological and professional resources to
support teachers, for instance, by planning new buildings towards
integrative methods, making available teaching aids, and developing
teachers' centres.

3. The movement towards greater collegial authority by such
means as rotation of leadership, open discussion of school policy,
and communication between neighbouring schools.

[24] Dearden, R. F., *The Philosophy of Primary Education* (Routledge & Kegan
Paul, 1968), p. 79.
[25] Lawton, Denis, 'The Idea of an Integrated Curriculum', in *Univ. of London
Institute of Education Bulletin*, Autumn, 1969.
[26] *Newsom Report* (HMSO, 1963), p. 126.

FURTHER READING

Birnie, Ian, *Religious Education in Integrated Studies* (SCM, 1972).

Brown, Mary and Precious, Norma, *The Integrated Day in the Primary School* (Ward Lock, 1968).

Chapman, Taylor R. and Clark, Harold V., *Thinking about Education: Introduction to Curriculum Studies in the Primary School* (Collins, 1968).

Davies, T. I., *School Organization: A New Synthesis* (Pergamon, 1969).

Dressel, P. L., 'The Meaning and Significance of Integration' in The Integration of Educational Experience, *National Society for the Study of Education, 57th Yearbook* (Univ. of Chicago, 1958).

Foster, John, *Discovery Learning in the Primary School* (Routledge & Kegan Paul, 1972).

Fraser, D. M., *Deciding What to Teach* (National Education Association, 1963).

Goodlad, J., *School Curriculum and the Individual* (Chicago Press, 1966).

Harris, A., *Thinking about Education* (Heinemann, 1970).

Hopkins, L. Thomas, *Integration: Its Meaning and Application* (Appleton Century, 1957).

Hubbard, Douglas, *Integrating Studies in the Primary School* (Sheffield Univ. 1970).

Huey, Francis J., *Teaching Primary Children* (Holt, Rinehart & Winston, 1965).

Jackson, P. W., *Life in Classrooms* (Holt, Rinehart & Winston, 1968).

King, A. R. and Brownell, J. A., *The Curriculum and the Disciplines of Knowledge* (John Wiley, 1966).

Komisar, B. Paul, '"Need" and the Needs-Curriculum', in Smith, B. O. and Ennis, R. H., *Language and Concepts in Education* (Rand McNally, 1961).

Lawton, Denis, 'The Idea of an Integrated Curriculum', in *London Institute of Education Bulletin*, Autumn 1969.

Maritain, J., *The Degrees of Knowledge* (G. Bles, 1959).

Miles, M. B., *Innovation in Education* (Columbia Teachers College, 1964).

Phenix, P. H., *Realms of Meaning* (McGraw Hill, 1964).

Rance, Peter, *Teaching by Topics* (Ward Lock, 1968).

Richmond, W. K., *The School Curriculum* (Methuen, 1970).

Rogers, Vincent, *Social Studies in Education* (Heinemann, 1968).

Smith, B. O., Stanley, W. O., and Shores, J. H., *Fundamentals of Curriculum Development* (Harcourt Brace, World Books, 1957).

Stenhouse, Lawrence, *Culture and Education* (Nelson, 1967).

Taba, Hilda, *Curriculum Development: Theory and Practice* (Harcourt Brace, 1962).

Taylor, Joy, *Organising and Integrating the Infant Day* (Allen & Unwin, 1971).

Taylor, Philip, *How Teachers Plan their Courses: Studies in Curriculum Planning* (NFER, 1970).

Tyler, R. W., *Basic Principles of Curriculum and Instruction* (Chicago Univ., 1969).

Walton, Jack, *The Integrated Day* (Ward Lock, 1971).

West, R. H., *Organisation in the Classroom* (Blackwell, 1967).

Wheeler, D. K., *Curriculum Process* (ULP, 1967).

Young, M. F. D., (ed.), *Knowledge and Control: New Directions for the Sociology of Education* (Collier Macmillan, 1971).

Chapter 11

Conclusion

Ten concepts have been considered as 'keys' to primary education but no attempt has been made to define a concept or to justify the preference for those chosen rather than others. The difficulty of definition may be illustrated by the opening discussion in which it was suggested that the best way of proceeding would be to outline the concept in terms of the educated person. Criteria such as membership of an élite or academic qualifications were rejected as being too narrow and because education is not synonymous with status or schooling. However, the attempt to define the distinguishing features of an educated person was no more successful; they were found to be infinite in number, degree and nature. Consequently, no sharp distinction was possible and although the concept did offer some classification it was not precise. There are always borderline cases, anomalies and matters of dispute.

Though a concept cannot be defined exactly or give an infallible classification its function is to construct a system of thought in which the various uses of the word are related. A concept cannot be pinned down but its analysis gives a framework within which practical decisions can be made with a measure of understanding. This is a matter of degree because in practice general principles cannot be applied directly. Suzanne Langer explains why, in our immediate confrontation with a practical situation, we do not proceed from a conceptual basis. 'It may seem strange that the most immediate experiences in our lives should be the least recognised, but there is a reason for this apparent paradox, and the reason is precisely their immediacy. They pass unrecorded because they are known without any symbolic mediation and therefore *without conceptual form*.'[1] Lack of precision in application is also due to the fact that no concept stands alone; though a system of thought it is not a self-contained one but is interlocked with others. Thus the concepts central to the child-centred view are inter-dependent. Activity is only educative if it includes experience but experience is only educative if it produces interest. Nor can the child-centred view

[1] Langer, Suzanne K., *Mind: An Essay on Human Feeling* (Johns Hopkins Press, 1967), p. 57. Quoted by Richmond, W. K., *The Free School* (Methuen, 1973), p. 13.

stand alone; it has to be related to the teacher-centred view in such concepts as initiation and evaluation. Concepts which stand in apparent opposition to each other must be brought together by other concepts such as co-operation, communication and integration.

So what has been attempted is a development of the concept of education by a series of concepts which also supplement each other. The actual words used are not vital to the argument because others could have been used in their place with equal relevance. Thus the following alternatives would have yielded much the same line of development.

Training	as	Instruction.
Initiation	as	Transmission.
Evaluation	as	Assessment.
Activity	as	Creativity.
Experience	as	Feeling.
Interest	as	Involvement.
Co-operation	as	Community
Communication	as	Relationship.
Integration	as	Unification.

Different words illuminate each other. Some are chosen because at a particular time they are 'in' words which have their day until supplanted by others. They acquire emotive associations because they are contrasted with others temporarily less in favour. Thus activity is contrasted with receptiveness, experience with memory, integration with fragmentation. Each contrast, however, throws some light on the meaning of the concept concerned. There can be no claim that a particular set of words are unique keys to the theory and practice of primary education; but the ideas behind them, taken as a whole and related to one another, do give a conceptual framework.

It might be considered by some that two vital concepts have been omitted, i.e. discipline and freedom. It could be that in emphasising the child-centred view too little attention has been given to the need for law and order or to the necessity that freedom in school should be well-regulated. The opposite argument is that it has been too readily assumed that education *must* take place in schools. Since learning can only take place through the initiative of the learner compulsory attendance at school necessarily involves repression, overt or covert, which negates the basic principle of education.

As to the first argument it could be said that due weight has been given to the teacher-centred view in which discipline is implied, and that its importance has been recognised throughout. Thus the discussion of the qualities of the good teacher laid stress on his capacity for organisation as the key to good order. Training necessarily involves repetition, automatic habit and the attainment of objective standards. Initiation by the teacher into worthwhile forms of knowledge is only possible if the learner submits to the disciplines involved. In evaluation there has to be an acceptance by both teacher and pupil of objective criteria of excellence to which both must submit. It must also include the diagnosis of the maladjusted minority who in every school are the major threat to the rule of law. Co-operation and communication between all the parties concerned, and especially between parents and teachers, are interpreted as essential for the development of self-discipline arising from an acceptance of moral values.

In general, primary school children are biddable if handled with reasonable tact and firmness though perhaps not enough is done to forestall the development of adolescent resistance later on. Teachers know that disorder is a rapidly spreading infection though in checking it they are in a dilemma. They are placed in authority but realise that an authoritarian stance is inimical to learning and that fruitful discipline must arise from the learning situation itself. Repression once established as the norm is difficult to reverse, despite the advice frequently given to young teachers to the contrary. The aim of discipline must be from the beginning not to assert a personal authority but to create a framework of habit within which individual differences can safely be tolerated. Madam Montessori is quoted as saying that her sole rule for children was that of good manners— admittedly she was to be the sole judge. The important thing is to establish a rule of law to which all, including the teacher, are bound but not a proliferation of rules difficult to enforce and irritating to obey. The criterion of success is whether the rule of law is self-perpetuating.

However, it is declared by some that such a framework is impossible where the people concerned have no option but to attend school. They see compulsory attendance as a denial of individual freedom. People who join a club or who enrol in a class do so voluntarily and thereby accept rules but children have to go to school willy-nilly. However unhappy they may be it is difficult even to change to another school. They may, indeed, play truant and this is causing concern in some cities, but by and large they are pressurised by parents and teachers to submit.

The reasons for legal compulsion are clear: the need to protect children from feckless or exploiting parents, to instil into children from the beginning a respect for authority, to ensure a minimum level of literacy, to keep children out of mischief, to provide an alternative to child labour. For the middle-class child there is no great problem. He accepts that going to school is natural. For the disadvantaged child it could be claimed with justice that school redresses his environmental handicaps. It gives him warmth, cleanliness, companionship and scope for activities. Yet one writer concludes a chapter on 'What's wrong with school anyway?' as follows, 'As applied in the past, legal compulsion may have served a useful purpose, In a less servile society, its retention is as anachronistic as that of corporal punishment. Until the education system is rid of it, schooling cannot be other than illiberal.'[2]

What arguments could be put forward to justify such a wholesale criticism of an institution, the school, on the grounds of compulsory attendance? First, it is said that schooling constrains its pupils physically and mentally. The bringing together of thirty or more children in a comparatively confined space is bound to have this effect. Second, schooling is only possible with standardised methods. Guided discovery and individual treatment are impossible in such conditions. Thirdly, the importance attached to literacy and to preparation for secondary education is bound to make school education 'seat-bound' and 'book-bound'. This may be acceptable for some children but certainly not for all. Finally the values inculcated in school are those which fit its organisation and which teachers understand as necessary for socialisation. Unfortunately they do not last for many children. Despite the widespread belief that schools have undergone a teaching revolution the fact is that they do not encourage independent learning; they inhibit it. Textbooks, workcards, assignments and all packaged learning materials prescribe for the child what to do. The school environment may be more relaxed than before but it is no less inimical to genuine learning.

Such an account certainly does not fit into any of the recent official reports. There it is acknowledged that there is room for improvement, but the impression given is that success lies just round the corner if certain reforms such as in-service training, teachers' centres, open-plan buildings and stages reorganisation are carried into effect. Nor does the criticism accord with the shining examples of what *can* be done in particular schools. In Oxfordshire, Leicestershire and the West Riding there are schools which have attracted attention from other parts of the world because they have demonstrated the possibilities of child-centred education. Indeed all over the country gifted and devoted teachers disprove the argument that state schools are necessarily restrictive.

Nevertheless, a few examples of excellence and a general lack of resentment in primary pupils does not prove that schools as a whole are providing an environment in which the natural curiosity of the

[2] Richmond, W. K., *The Free School* (Methuen, 1973), p. 90.

average child is fully awakened or satisfied. But what are the alternatives? Is 'de-schooling' a viable answer? Attempts have been made in this country and elsewhere to establish so-called 'free schools', i.e. schools outside the state system, where attendance is voluntary and there is no imposed curriculum and where parents, indeed the whole community, are closely involved, As an example the Scotland Road Free School in Liverpool may be mentioned. It opened in June 1971 in a typical 'down-town' area with about forty pupils aged from 6 to 16. According to its prospectus it 'does not seek to impose its own values, but has as its premise a total acceptance of the people and the area'. It depends for its running on voluntary contributions, many of them raised in the local community, but it still cannot pay its full-time teachers some of whom have to depend on social security.

What is remarkable about ventures such as Scotland Road is that it represents an effort by an educationally deprived area to find its own solution to the problem of what to do with the young. It is an alternative to the educational priority arrangements proposed by *Plowden*. Whether it will last is doubtful. Whether it has anything of lasting value to offer to the state system is an open question. The problem is whether the state should abandon or modify its monopolistic claims to be the sole provider of education. In Denmark tentative moves have been made to link public financial strength with local and private initiative. In that country education is compulsory but not necessarily in state schools. If a group of parents can combine together to provide an alternative which meets minimum requirements then financial support will be given for at least 85 per cent of the cost. So in various places, mostly middle-class, so-called 'little schools' have been set up. The most important feature is that parents and teachers are in genuine partnership. Parents come into the school freely at all times and take a full share in the planning of the curriculum. The emphasis is on creativity, on the arts, on group activities and shared experiences. The small numbers (100 or less) make possible a very relaxed and informal régime so that the school becomes, in fact, an extended neighbourhood family. The question arises whether some such arrangement would not meet many of the criticisms of the 'de-schoolers'.

Certain concepts and the ideas which they express have been spoken of as 'keys' to primary education. Perhaps it could be suggested that though they may unlock the doors it is necessary for all concerned—teachers, administrators, parents, the general public, even the children—to take possession of the building.

FURTHER READING

Alves, C., *Schooling in the Middle Years* (Macmillan, 1973).
Ball, C. M., *Education for a Change* (Penguin, 1973).
Blishen, Edward, *The School that I'd like* (Penguin, 1969).
Charles, Betty, *The Community School* (87a Borough High Street, London, S.E.1, 1971).
Goodman, Paul, *Compulsory Miseducation* (Penguin, 1971).
Holt, John, *What Do I Do Monday* (Pitman, 1970).
Illich, Ivan, *Deschooling Society* (Penguin, 1973).
Mays, J. B., *Education and the Urban Child* (Liverpool Univ. 1962).
Midwinter, Eric, *Social Environment and the Urban Child* (Ward Lock, 1972).
Midwinter, Eric, *Patterns of Community Education* (Ward Lock, 1973).
Musgrove, F. T., *Patterns of Power and Responsibility in English Education* (Methuen, 1971).
Reimer, Everett, *School is Dead* (Penguin, 1971).
Richmond, W. K., *The Free School* (Methuen, 1973).
Shipman, M., *Education and Modernisation* (Faber, 1971).
Taylor, L. C., *Resources for Learning* (Penguin, 1971).

Index